HOW TO TALK ~~TO~~ *with* TEENAGERS

G. Wade Rowatt, Jr.

BROADMAN PRESS
NASHVILLE, TENNESSEE

For Ashley,
my next teenager

© Copyright 1990 ● Broadman Press
All rights reserved
4254-46
ISBN: 0-8054-5446-2
Dewey Decimal Classification: 306.8
Subject Heading: FAMILY // ADOLESCENCE
Library of Congress Catalog Card Number: 90-34772
Printed in the United States of America

Unless otherwise indicated, Scripture is from the *Revised Standard Version of the Bible* copyright 1946, 1952, © 1971, 1973 by the National Council of the Churches of Christ in the U.S.A., and used by permission. References marked KJV are from the *King James Version.*

Publisher's Note: Footnotes are in parentheses in the text. Refer to bibliography for complete footnote information.

Library of Congress Cataloging-in-Publication Data
Rowatt, Wade.
   How to talk with teenagers / G. Wade Rowatt, Jr.
      p. cm. — (The Bible and personal crisis)
   Includes bibliographical references.
   ISBN 0-8054-5446-2
   1. Teenagers—Pastoral counseling of. 2. Teenagers—Religious
life. 3. Storytelling in Christian education. I. Title.
II. Series.
BV4447.R68 1990
259'.23—dc20

90-34772
CIP

Acknowledgments

The ideas for this book fermented for a number of years. Some bright ideas sparkled for a moment but evaporated under closer scrutiny. Other ideas fermented but seemed to turn sour. This book represents a distillation of ideas tested through formal and informal conversations with a wide range of colleagues. Youth ministers, pastors, seminary professors, and pastoral counselors have all added to the mix. But the real test for the concepts in this volume have been adolescents themselves. Numerous hours of talking with adolescents in groups and quietly in my office have led to the conviction that storytelling is a powerful medium for communicating with teens.

This volume reaches publication with many debts owed to both individuals and institutions. The publishers of *event* magazine gave me an opportunity for ten years to write a monthly dialogue column with teenagers. This task pushed me to fashion and refashion numerous stories. Churches have provided a variety of contexts in which to attempt to minister to youth. Each church that has permitted me an opportunity of ministry contributed to this volume. Dr. Roy L. Honeycutt and the seminary where I teach have provided administrative support and resources for the preparation of the manuscript.

Edward Thornton's invitation to "write a book on communicating with teenagers" led me to the task of bringing these ideas together between the front and back covers. His personal encouragement, professional editorial assistance, and his own journey of faith sustained me through this process. Keitha Brasler has labored long hours as manuscript assistant in preparing this volume. Were it not for her cheerful dedication to the task and her sacrificial giving of her time, these ideas would never have appeared in print.

My own family has shouldered more than their share of the household responsibilities while I have written these lines. My loving wife, Jodi, has taken on extra responsibilities in our two-career marriage so that I might be freed for the task of writing. As always, my ministry is enriched by her care and support. Brock and Wade were teenagers when this volume began, but they turned twenty during the process of writing. They have been living stories of faith pilgrimage, and I shall remain thankful to God for their teaching me about adolescents as only one's children can. Ashley, age nine at the time of the writing of this volume, is my next teenager. She has contributed by sharing her many, many stories to encourage me in the process of writing.

Special thanks go to the youth who have invited me into their lives as a caring friend and professional counselor. As we have journeyed together in search of ourselves, we have indeed become soul mates, friends across the generation. Their stories have become my story; the gospel story has become our story. I thank God for the privilege of walking through a journey of time at their side.

G. Wade Rowatt, Jr.
January 1990

Contents

Introduction

Multitudes of parents fill my ears with a common complaint. Perhaps you hear the same. "My teenagers simply won't talk with me. When they do speak, I can't get anything out of them." Parents come up after lectures, fathers and mothers stop to talk after presentations at church, counselees plead for help on the telephone. A wide variety of parents recognize the communication barrier between them and their adolescent offspring. They complain: "I tried to ask my teenagers what's wrong, and I got the same answer: a mumbled 'oh, nothing.' When I inquire about their opinions, they moan something like 'I don't care.' And when I try to ask for specific information, all I get is 'I don't know.' " Youth workers and teachers recite similar stories.

This generation gap appears to be widespread. It doesn't have to be that way. Some parents and teenagers communicate quite effectively. Certain adults demonstrate an ease at reaching out to youth. Many do not. However, this is not a new problem; adolescents and parents for generations have experienced a wall between them. Even Aristotle is reported to have complained that the younger generation was going to the dogs and lacked respect for their elders. Most likely, a part of the difficulty between Paul and young John Mark was the generation gap issue. The counterculture revolution of the sixties was marked by ineffective communication between the generations. Teachers, pastors, parents, and other professionals all found themselves locked out of adolescent communication circles.

A recent inquiry from a youth minister painfully illustrates the communication dilemma. The early-twenties youth minister saw herself as quite effective and imagined she was very close with the teenagers in her youth group. Certainly the success as measured by the growth of the group would indicate she was well liked. She was shocked and nearly devastated when the female president of the youth group turned up pregnant. The young lady had difficulty in talking with her youth minister about it. Even when communication seems somewhat effective, a crisis in an adolescent's life tests the limits of the communication. From the youth's viewpoint, there is a failure to trust that adequate communication will happen. Many times, they simply don't believe adults will understand. They fear rejection and in their anxiety retreat into silence.

Scott, a bright, attractive sixteen year old, had spent three days in an adolescent unit of a psychiatric hospital. He refused to communicate with anyone other than to ask for food and to refuse treatment. He had attempted suicide for the third time within six months. He would not discuss why. The fact that he had left no note was a loud communication that he wanted to remain silent on the subject. Numerous professionals on the hospital staff, from the psychiatric aide, to the nurse, to the psychiatrist, to the medical resident, to the social worker, to the family therapist, to the art therapist, had all tried and failed to reach Scott. He simply would not talk.

While there are no easy answers for parents, ministers, and other professionals who wish to communicate with teenagers, there is hope; and some principles and experiences can be utilized to reach adolescents. The pages that follow are not so much a how-to as they are a road map. While these will not teach you to drive, hopefully they will provide a sense of direction and a sense of travel dialogue that will make your journey into sharing with youth more meaningful, effective, and perhaps even enjoyable.

Purpose

The idea for this book came from the mother of one of my teenage friends. I had been counseling for nearly a year with her son. He had invested energy in growing and had demonstrated courage in risking depth dialogue with me. His story has served as an inspiration for me to continue to reach out to troubled teens. However, it was a phone call from his mother that inspired this attempt to help others know how to talk with teenagers. She called one Friday afternoon, asking for a referral for her younger son. She said, "Wade, I need someone to talk to my other son the same way that you talk to Brett. I need someone to tell him the kind of stories that you tell. Brett's always repeating them. It can't be you because Brett has shared so much about you, and this problem relates to conflict between the two of them." In reflecting on my list of customary referrals, I became aware that only a few stated that they were comfortable in talking with teenagers. Some of my professional friends counseled exclusively with adults. Others do an excellent job of relating to teens, so I suggested one.

I proposed soon after to write this volume in order to assist pastors, parents, professional counselors, and other helping professionals to communicate more effectively with adolescents. While certainly many of the illustrations will focus on youth in crisis, it is my hope that this book will assist adults to communicate with adolescents at a level that will prevent many of the more severe crises all too common in the contemporary adolescent world.

Preventive care is the least expensive, most effective intervention with adolescents. Effective communication can assist teenagers in finding alternatives before their struggle becomes a catastrophe. In my experience of over twenty years in counseling youth I have become convinced that most adolescent crises are misdirected attempts to meet legitimate needs. A young lady who feels a need for intimacy may wind up pregnant. A lonely teenage boy may soon turn to substance abuse in order to forget his loneliness or to find acceptance from peers who are already users. A teenager may run away in order to escape excruciating and hopeless problems between her and her parents. All too often teenagers jump out of the frying pan into the fire trying to resolve issues that could be helped if more effective communication existed between them and the adults in their lives.

A secondary purpose of this book is to deepen the reader's appreciation for teenagers and their situation in society. While more than a little fun is poked at today's adolescents, their plight is far from humorous. Today's teenagers, for the most part, receive negative billing in movies, television, and music. They are most frequently pictured as immature, impulsive, uncaring, angry, and radical. While there certainly are enough teenagers to warrant this description, such a group in my experience would be in the minority. There is a large number of bright, committed, dedicated, honest, albeit searching adolescents in today's world. Any disillusionment concerning youth should be at least partially dispelled by the reading of these pages. In interviewing teenagers across the United States, I have been impressed with the sincerity of their search, their responsiveness when offered opportunities for help, and their commitment to build a better world.

In particular, I remember Tracy, a seventeen-year-old, who after a tumultuous, traumatic early adolescence has worked hard to help her single mother survive economic pressures. She works an average of thirty hours a week while maintaining honor-roll grades through her junior and senior years of high school. She has an active social life and a searching, growing commitment to her faith. I can wish for every reader an opportunity to know Tracy and her commitment to be all she can be through the grace of God.

I hope this volume will provide readers with a number of stories, incidents, cases, and vignettes of life to be used in their own reaching out to youth. While these stories have been changed enough to protect the identity of the youth, their letters, phone calls, and confessions have provided the substance. They reflect authentic situations. I have found that telling stories is an effective way to make my points. Frequently, adolescents will highlight a dynamic of a story that goes well beyond the initial intent of the storyteller. If these stories are as productive for you as they have been for me, rich dialogues will follow between you and the teenagers in your life.

A final purpose of this volume is to sketch out pictures of the faith struggle of contemporary teens. I will not discuss the structure of adolescent faith; rather I provide portraits of faith at work in the lives of teens. If through the reading of these pages you catch something of the shape, the color, the hues, the contrast, and the composition of the portraits of the faith struggle of teens, then the book has achieved its purpose. All of us will see some of ourselves and certainly recall rich moments (and perhaps dark hours) from our faith pilgrimage as youth. However, we need to take caution not to project our pilgrimage on the youth with whom we minister. As their spiritual guides, you will be in their picture. Take care that it remains *their* picture.

Methods

A pastoral, theological method undergirds the research for this work. The dialogue between the incidents presented by youth and their families and biblical, theological material has resulted in the theoretical framework behind the stories presented herein. The process begins with the presentation of an issue in the life of a teenager. For example, a teenager presents a dilemma, such as seeing a teacher cheat at school, and asks what should be done. As the issue is dissected, several dynamics surface. For example, the nature of authority, the commitment to truth, and the trust that negative repercussions would not result all surface in the case. One by one, the issues are studied from a biblical perspective and subjected to theological scrutiny. A large number of conclusions may be reached from such a massive data-collecting process. For example, one would need to ask what are biblical teachings on the nature of authority. How do these fit together into a theological whole? As each issue is explored, one returns to the Bible to pick up the next, until all obvious issues have been closely examined. Then one asks, "What does this massive data indicate are appropriate alternatives in response to the dilemma?" For example, this student and adult helper might say that ultimate authority lies with God, that the teacher's authority over the student while certainly demanding respect would not call on the student to join in the dishonesty. However, the student might realistically face repercussions. A number of choices might be offered to the student, but ultimately the student would have to decide for herself or himself.

The method does not stop with having reached a conclusion or selected an alternative. The reflection process reverses as the helper asks the student what the case then teaches about his or her understanding of God, Scripture, and how that understanding might be enlarged from this experience. More specifically, one would ask the student after the incident, "What have you learned about yourself and your faith as a result of this experience?" Such a method has guided me through numerous conversations with teenagers. While not all experiences have been productive, all have been inspirational.

The data for this work grows out of a number of previous writing assignments for adolescents, their families, and professionals who work with them. For over ten years, I wrote a monthly column in a religious, adolescent leisure-reading magazine: *event*. Frequently, the nature of the article was a story built around a letter, a phone call, or a question from a teenager. Many of the stories in this volume build on the stories in the column, "Jean-age Reflections," from *event* magazine. *Ministry with Youth and Their Families,* a joint venture of myself and Dr. Richard Ross, a youth consultant with my denomination, has provided foundational concepts for understanding the dynamics of adolescent society and, in particular, the families of adolescents. A more recent work, *Pastoral Care with Youth in Crisis,* has provided specific data that undergirds my understanding of the scope of crises facing today's youth. With the assistance of a Lily Foundation grant, the material for that volume was collected by sending questionnaires to five ministers, five youth ministers, and five counselors in each of the fifty states. I traveled across the United States, interviewing teenagers and youth ministers, and talking with their teachers, parents, and pastors. For nine months, I served as a consultant on the adolescent psychiatric unit of Norton Hospital in Louisville, Kentucky. All of this data serves as foundational background for this book.

At the foundation of an understanding of adolescents, this volume rests on the Bible. While the terms *adolescent* and *teenager* are nowhere to be found in Scripture—children were considered adults when they turned thirteen—the terms *young man, young woman*, and *youth* are found frequently. There are many biblical stories of persons who most likely were between thirteen and twenty years of age—David, Absalom, Joseph, Jesus, and John Mark. Eutychus, Ruth, Esther, and Mary, the mother of Jesus, were most likely all teenagers. We will return frequently to these accounts for our understanding of the stories of the adolescents in our world.

Overview

The story of today's teen is mixed with celebration and sadness. We celebrate the teenagers whose lives are a testimony to goodness. We celebrate with many spiritually mature youth in our churches. We celebrate the academic excellence, athletic development, musical achievements, and many other talents of the youth of the world.

Nevertheless, there is a note of sadness as we look at the story of today's teenagers because of the number of problems they face. American teenagers have the highest suicide rate, substance abuse rate, and pregnancy rate of any Western civilized nation. The problems they face are frequently deadly. Their crises reflect a great number of dynamics. It is not atypical for teenagers to have school problems, conflicts with parents, substance abuse, and depression—all at one time.

As we look at communicating with teenagers, we will focus on the art of storytelling, and different types of stories will be explored as alternatives for reaching out to all kinds of teens. One must reach out to growing teens in order to sustain their growth, just as one reaches out to teens in a crisis in order to minister to their needs.

Case studies and stories are an effective way of assisting teenagers to understand their own values as well as to encourage them to think biblically about the decisions they face. While there are a number of adolescents making bad decisions, an even larger number are making good decisions—but for the wrong reasons. In adolescent value clashes with parents, effective communication is the essential that heightens the possibility for productive resolution. Teens and their parents who can talk about value differences stand a better chance of making it through to productive living. Frequently adolescents will refer to their own life situation as "something out of an unbelievable soap opera." Their living stories are frequently more bizarre than those concocted for entertainment purposes. Assisting youth in telling their story can be an effective beginning for the counseling process. Helping them understand the gospel story and its implication for their lives provides an excellent resource for growth.

Not infrequently, adolescents' stories are filled with missing data and seemingly contradictory facts. Young persons, while not always deliberately misrepresenting the truth, represent the truth from their perspective. It is important for adults who are assisting teens in life's adjustments to understand the process of gathering data from adolescents. Simply stated, adults need to help teenagers reflect responsibly on their stories as well as future decisions.

Generation after generation of adolescent development has brought teens to their present experiences. Teenagers are frequently unaware of the adolescent stories of their parents, grandparents, and great-grandparents. However, these family stories in powerful ways fashion their young lives. Introducing teenagers to the stories of their parents and grandparents and helping the parents and grandparents to understand the teen's story can lead to great blessings for the family.

Peer pressure remains the number one shaping force for youth. Stories of their friends may take on "living legend" dimensions and lure teenagers into behaviors that otherwise would be quickly rejected.

Adolescents frequently do not understand their own feelings. Stories that help them articulate their feelings and manage those feelings responsibly can be productive for their growth. A wide variety of feelings interrupt the adolescent's world daily. Assisting in the expression and positive resolution of such feelings remains a paramount issue in helping youth in crisis.

Adolescents are in a faith pilgrimage. The gospel story, intertwined with their own story, provides powerful forces to effect change.

A Story for Teens

The following story is offered for the readers, in whatever fashion they wish to share it with teenagers. Perhaps you would like to use sections of this material in your conversations or speeches with teenagers. You may want to use part of it in a newsletter, a brochure, or circular inviting and introducing teenagers to your outlook. Use it, change it, modify it, make it yours.

What is a teenager? You might ask why adults ask such silly questions in the first place. No one seems to get really excited about describing a thirty- or forty-year-old? So what's so big about teenagers?

Children are promised great things when they become teens. Middle-aged persons like to talk about when they were teens. They remember stories of fourteen- or sixteen- or eighteen-year-old triumphs. Even grandparents remember their special times as young people. You know that technically a teenager is anyone over twelve and under the age of twenty. But perhaps you do not know a lot of other things about being a teenager. Actually, I like the term *jean-ager*. To me, it means "easygoing, laid-back, fun loving, relaxed, and most of all, real." These words also describe teenagers for me. But "jean-ager" calls attention to the differentness. I suppose a teenager really is anyone on the road between childhood and adulthood. A teenager is a boy becoming a man or a girl becoming a woman. By that definition, many eleven- and twelve-year-olds are already teenagers. But some twenty-year-olds or even twenty-five-year-olds can still be adolescents.

If a teenager is someone changing from a child into a grown-up, what are those changes? You know that a tadpole loses its tail, grows legs, and one day becomes a frog. A frog continues swimming but begins jumping. A caterpillar loses its many legs, sheds its wormlike skin, grows wings, and one day becomes a butterfly. That "worm" stops crawling about awkwardly and becomes a fanciful, fluttering insect dancing from flower to flower. Tadpoles hide in underwater weeds until they are through changing. Caterpillars spin a cocoon for their changing closet. But teenagers grow up right out in the open. That makes it infinitely more difficult. Really, each jean-ager needs a room for himself or herself—a place to hide when the changes seem too embarrassing. Teenagers need privacy.

What about those changes? Like tadpoles and caterpillars, teens lose some things too. Children let go of things in order to start becoming adults. Like frogs and butterflies, teens do grow some new parts as they are becoming adults. The transformation is dramatic.

Teens begin letting go of many things. They let go of their parents' thoughts and start thinking for themselves. What does it mean to be a thinking jean-ager? For one thing, it means making decisions for oneself. Beginning to think through problems on one's own, having personal ideas, and learning to make good decisions are an important part of letting go of parents' ways of thinking. This may mean teens doing things their own way, being their own person. But this does not mean forgetting the rules and running wild. A child can do that. Thinking for oneself does mean being responsible, but it doesn't mean being different just to be different. It means using one's mind and making decisions on one's own.

Somewhere in the growing process, teens start letting go of their parents' money too. Earning their own money is an important part of growing up. This means finding a way and a place for a job. Youth want to have their own things. They really understand that things are theirs when they are making their own money. Teens who buy their own clothes, books, radios, and perhaps even a phone, a TV, or a car have a sense of personal identity. As they begin letting go of their parents' money, they find a new sense of self.

The sooner youth start making their own money, the quicker they grow up. Granted, finding a way to make money isn't easy, and certainly deciding on a career can be very confusing. But as teenagers begin to let go of their parents' money, they begin the process of learning to support themselves.

Usually, earning money means letting go of something else: free time. Children do have more time to play than teens. Be careful, teenager, that you don't let go of *all* of this fun time. Don't get too busy too soon! Teenagers need time to make and enjoy friends. They need time to reflect on decisions. They need a moratorium, a time-out from their busy life to process growing up. They need a time to be alone, to daydream, and to meditate. They need a time for spiritual nourishment.

Teenagers are even letting go of something very personal—their skin. That babylike covering that children have keeps transforming itself into a tough hide for adult living. Actually, a youth's skin starts to grow up. This may mean more oil, more sweat, more hair, and, unfortunately, more blemishes. As teenagers literally develop adult skin, they need to also develop an adult stance toward the world.

As children journey to adulthood through the transition of adolescence, they let go of simple thinking. Adolescents need to reflect on the complexities of the world around them. New issues dominate their thinking. Youth can begin to think seriously about war and peace, love and marriage, pollution and environmental protection, world hunger and overeating. These new issues take the place of playing house or building models or pursuing board games. Teenagers let go of thinking like children and start to think, act, and feel like mature persons. They can say as Paul said in 1 Corinthians 13:11: "When I was a child, I spoke like a child, I thought like a child, I reasoned like a child; when I became [an adult], I gave up childish ways."

Letting go can be rather sad. But usually this is not so with teens because there are so many new things to replace the old. Most teens do not grieve losing their childhood. A few do.

Teens acquire many new things to replace what they lose in the letting go of childhood. They get new bodies, new friends, new brains, and have new feelings. They have new breaks and new opportunities in life. Hopefully, they develop a new, rich, and growing faith. Their new bodies may seem strange at first. A youth looks in a mirror and hardly recognizes himself or herself. Knowing what to expect is a big help in accepting the physiological changes. Parents and teachers need to warn them far in advance about the physical changes. Of course, each individual teen unfolds at his or her own rate. Help them to be patient. Try to help them understand that their time for growing up physically will arrive.

New friends are often made during teenage years. As youth become more active and travel in wider social circles, they have more opportunities to meet other youth. They should be encouraged to nurture these friendships. Teenagers may have one or two best friends, but they need four, five, or six good buddies and "just friends." Friends help youth to grow up and not overly depend on their parents. They also help in sad, frightening, painful, and angry times.

Youth seem to have a new brain as they develop the capability to think abstract thoughts. They can see complicated relationships, perhaps even find algebra understandable. Teens can see for the first time some of their parents' weaknesses and some of the ambiguities in the adult world around them. Their new brain is a powerful tool, and they are to be encouraged to use it wisely and with discipline. Education and skill training deserve primary attention.

New feelings rush through the teenagers' bodies like lightening cracking across a cloud-darkened sky. Youth wake up to urges and forces deep within themselves. These feelings are more often than not directed toward members of the opposite sex. They need adults to assist them in understanding the power of a multitude of feelings. Their feelings rise and fall like the lead car of a roller coaster—frequently for no apparent reason. One minute they might be dominated by shame and guilt or by hurt and frustration; a moment later they will be filled with excitement, love, and on the edge of hysteria. Youth need to be encouraged to talk about their feelings. They are fortunate if parents, ministers, teachers, and others can hear them out and assist them in identifying, labeling, and focusing feelings. Unresolved feelings can make their lives miserable, but shared feelings can lead them on a rewarding journey into new levels of intimacy.

Teens get a lot of new breaks. They find new opportunities in many first-time experiences. Some undisciplined youth will try anything at least once. While this may sound like fun, it can lead to tragedy. Not everything is worth trying, even once. Wise youth not only learn from their experiences, but they also learn from watching the mistakes of others. Youth have many new roads to travel as teenagers—their first date, their first job, and their first opportunity to drive an automobile. Assist them to make wise decisions.

A new faith also grows in the jean-age years. The simple faith of childhood may be refreshing and joyful, but few youth find it satisfactory for the challenges they face. As the young Jesus grew in wisdom and stature, so must their faith. Youth must begin to develop a mature faith that goes beyond the milk of childhood to the meat of deep Bible study. As youth cast aside the simplicities of their childhood faith, they must be challenged to grow spiritually. A mentor, spiritual guide, or discipleship trainer will mean much in their lives. They will need assistance in nurturing their faith. Adults will need to be comfortable with candid, honest discussions and open, depth Bible study if they expect spiritual disciplines to grow in the youth around them. Undoubtedly, the youth will face doubts. Rather than hide them, straightforward, frank confrontation, and turning to the Scriptures will more likely bring spiritual growth.

Yes, being a jean-ager means letting go of childhood and getting a handle on adulthood. Youth are alive and growing. The transformation years are the most important years of growth. Adolescents need adult guidance in order to decide when to let go of something and when to hold on. Thank God for the process of adolescence. Thank God if you are a jean-ager.

1

The Story of Today's Teens

Whatever else adolescence may be, it is certainly a time for dreams, romantic ideals, and fantasies. Youthful enthusiasm, optimism, and hope have dominated the teen years for generations. Each new wave of jean-agers devises ways of transforming their world, of growing up, but seldom thinks of growing old. While no one wants to shatter the optimistic dreams of adolescents, if permitted to go unchecked their fantasy worlds soon crash.

Contemporary adolescents face a complex world of nuclear missiles, unstable governments, historic political breakthroughs, medical miracles, space travel, economic revolutions, overnight millionaires, starving street people, molested children, kidnapped youth, overcrowded prisons, and a multitude of other complexities. While the problems facing contemporary youth are unparalleled in their magnitude, so perhaps are the possibilities they encounter. Youth of the 1990s will perhaps undergo a counterculture revolution more sophisticated, perhaps less rebellious, but similar to that of the 1920s and the 1960s. Today's youth do face a multitude of unanswered questions, but their prospects for the future remain bright. As we support today's youth, we contribute to their story of the next generation.

Talking About Problems

Most often, adolescents whose lives are in turmoil do not personally seek out help. They are referred by a friend, parent, or institution, for a variety of reasons.

Identity Crisis

In a recent survey of adolescent crises, identity formation remained a number one concern among those who work with youth (Rowatt, 14). A significant portion of adolescents feel unacceptable physically, socially, and intellectually. The grass always seems browner on the side of the fence that bears their name. They look in a mirror and cringe at the comparison of their own faces, skin, hair, and body to the enhanced images of teenagers they see in movies and on television. They know they don't quite measure up. They feel unconfirmed in their own identity.

Teens keep this awful secret ("I don't like the way I look.") from their closest friends and perhaps even their parents. They often assume they are the only ones who feel so ugly, so unacceptable, so awful, or so clumsy. Even those who win beauty contests privately report feelings of self-doubt. Adolescence is perhaps the time of lowest confidence in one's physical self-image. Youth are so vulnerable that the least put-down or attack on their physiological self causes suffering.

Few youth can live up to the social expectations of the teen environment. The media broadcasts an idealized, romanticized world where using brand-name items brings instant social success. Cliques form in the schools, and all members worry about their rank in the social order. Even those who are seen at the top of the social ladder by others feel the fragility of their positions and worry about social acceptance. While girls perhaps dominate boys in the amount of anxiety expressed over social acceptance, the fears of not fitting in are in no way limited to the female gender. Teenage boys frequently report loneliness, ostracism, and a lack of depth relationships with other males. Both groups feel the social pressure of not having a special boyfriend or girlfriend, and yet few adolescents can find meaningful dating relationships. The mobility of society, the unrealistic expectations from the media, and the lack of appropriate gathering places for adolescents all lead to deterioration of the adolescent social structure. This deterioration intensifies feelings of alienation, isolation, estrangement, and fears of being a social outcast, derelict, or exile.

Worldwide pressure forces a nation's education system to produce the brightest scientists, economists, and artistic thinkers possible. As leaders scurry to compare their educational systems, adolescents' performance in schools is compared nationally, like athletes' performance in the Olympics. No country wants to come up short in the brain trust area. Adolescents keenly feel the pressure to perform academically. The pressure to be the very best causes many of them to miss sight of their own level of giftedness, talents, and perhaps nonintellectual abilities. A large portion of American youth are giving up in despair. The high school drop-out rate is higher than ever. Once the youth begin to feel dumb, they cease to perform to their own level of potential. Vocational training has received such negative publicity that some youth feel uncomfortable with it. Many want into the very best universities.

The tragedy of the pressure of academic performance is perhaps best captured in the story of a young Asian-American lady who attempted suicide because she had made a *B* on her report card. Even the most intellectually gifted adolescents are not gifted in every area and feel a sense of negative identity intellectually. Recapturing a sense of the unique blessing of different gifts as shared by Paul in 1 Corinthians 12 is at the heart of assisting adolescents in dealing with the problem of negative identity based on performance. "Now there are diversities of gifts, but the same Spirit. And there are differences of administrations, but the same Lord" (1 Cor. 12:4-5, KJV). We need to help our teens see that each of them is a unique gift to their world. To paraphrase a popular book of the sixties, they need to feel that they are OK and their peers are OK, not as a blind denial of imperfections but as a joyous gift of grace in the goodness of God's creation.

Loneliness

A second problem facing today's adolescents is loneliness. Natural peer groups that formed around stable neighborhood groupings deteriorated with the urbanization of America. More youth are separated at school, at church, and by a variety of activities. Teens repeatedly answer "no one" when asked, "Who is your best friend?" Of course, loneliness and lack of friends are not new among young persons. The shifts in peer groups caused by varied rates of development, new activities, changing interests, and new friendships developing around the mobility of a vehicle have left some adolescents standing on the sidelines for some time. In the early 1970s Merton Strommen conducted a study of high school age youth. He found that over half felt concerned that their classmates at school were not friendly enough and were inconsiderate of their feelings (Strommen, 22).

Brad is typical of such youth. A high school junior no longer able to play football because of a knee injury, Brad found it difficult to make new friends. He was depressed and acting out at church. In his first interview with me, one of his statements was, "Nobody likes me." "How do you know?" I inquired. "Because when I greet them, they don't even speak back at school. Nobody." I confronted his all-or-nothing thinking by saying that certainly somebody would speak to him. I asked him to keep a record for one week, each day recording the number of classmates to whom he spoke and the number who returned his greetings. To his surprise, nearly 55 percent of his classmates did return his greetings. I must confess I was a bit taken aback that over 45 percent did not. Loneliness and isolation are real problems for today's youth. After a time of self-discovery, Brad bonded with new friends, but his kind numbers millions.

Conflict with Parents

A third major issue facing contemporary youth is perhaps as old as parenthood. Teens still have frequent conflicts with their parents. Granted that the number of youth with single parents and stepfamilies has increased, it is doubtful that the total number of parent-youth tensions, differences, and conflicts has increased over the generations. Parents and teenagers who do not deal with the adolescent's need for independence and development of a self-identity are doomed to unproductive disagreements. The Bible clearly states that youth are to leave their father and mother as they cleave to their new mate. It seems evident that this event cannot be pinpointed precisely. It does not occur overnight. The process of leaving needs to begin early in the adolescent's identity formation. As adolescents are capable of making decisions and caring for themselves, wise parents reduce the conflict by loosening the apron strings. Parent-youth conflicts are most destructive in closed family systems. Families that do not interact with other families in society and are not open to interchanges with social structures (schools, churches, community activities, and athletic teams) are less open to change. They are not as tolerant of the growing up of their teenagers. As they build a wall around their family system, trying to insulate their teenager from the world, they are more likely to push their teenager into rebellion and perhaps a crisis.

Parents would do well to remember not only the anxiety of the mother of Jesus when they had traveled two days and He was not in their midst, but also the permission that she gave Him when He was found and informed her, "I must be about my Father's business" (Luke 2:49, KJV). Each person is created with unique gifts. Adolescence is a time for developing those gifts and pulling away from the parents' authority. Independence does not mean emotional distance. In fact, intimacy grows in the context of mutual respect.

Substance Abuse

A fourth crisis facing teenagers is substance abuse. While evidence points to a slight decline in the latter part of the 1980s in the overall drug use among American teenagers, the United States still maintains the highest rate of illicit drug use of any civilized country. Adolescents take drugs for a variety of reasons, but the major reason for that first experience is introduction through a peer group or a young adult friend. Others are seeking excitement, escape from hopelessness, or simply experimenting for a good time. While stopping the importation and production of hard drugs is certainly important, helping youth meet their psychosocial and spiritual needs would be a giant step toward keeping them off drugs. For drug-free adolescents, we need to help them to say no by giving them attractive alternatives to which they can say yes.

Obviously effective antidrug education is important in stopping the illicit drug usage. However, churches can assist further by strengthening the families of adolescents. Furthermore, providing a safe place in which teens can pursue activities and find a degree of excitement creates a positive environment.

Cindy, a fourteen-year-old high school freshman, had been using marijuana and experimenting with some hard drugs for nearly a year when her mother brought her to me for assistance. Her difficulties started several years earlier as she struggled to adjust to her parents' divorce and her father's remarriage to a girl only seven years her senior. Cindy had been introduced to drugs by a friend after school. With focused family counseling, appropriate medical help, and an opportunity for her to develop new friends, Cindy was able to turn from her drug experimentation and become an honor student again. Endless hours of time were invested by Cindy's family, teachers, and concerned individuals, but all said that her turnaround was worth it. A unified, systems response can work.

Sexual Problems

A fifth concern facing today's teenagers, sexual problems, is frequently mentioned as the greatest pressure by a number of adolescents. Teenagers' sexual problems usually have their beginning in early childhood. When children fail to receive adequate sex education and positive reinforcement for who they are as boys and girls, they are programmed for sexual confusion and acting out. Teenagers who receive accurate sexual information and clear value training about their sexuality from their parents are less likely to have sexual crises.

A society that sells everything from deodorant to automobiles using sex as the lure is bound to have difficulties with adolescent sexual problems. Young persons cannot be expected to wade through the barrage of sexual misinformation and temptations without clear guidance from the adults in their world. If the churches and the homes do not provide adequate sex education, it is difficult for other institutions to take over this task exclusively.

The variety of adolescent sex problems seems to be increasing at an alarming rate. Adolescent pregnancies are on the increase, adolescent abortions are on the increase, the number of sexually abused youth is on the increase, sexual promiscuity among teenagers is on the increase, and sex education in our churches seems to be on the decrease.

A number of adolescents confuse sexual acts with love. The need to love and to be loved appears universal, not only among youth but among all persons. Mother Teresa, known for her commitment to feeding the world's hungry, has said that hunger is not only for a piece of bread; hunger is for love and for being wanted (Mother Teresa, 82). Youth want to be loved, and they give sex to get what they think is love. While it is understandable that many parents and church workers are concerned about adolescent sexual behavior, we need to be just as concerned about the unmet needs that fuel some of that behavior. Teaching appropriate behavior is the first step, but assisting youth to meet their spiritual and emotional needs must follow suit.

An equal concern of some teenagers is the attitude not only toward sex but toward sexuality. Adolescent males and females show a growing level of concern for the put-downs and abuse that they feel as they live in a sex-biased society. One fifteen year old shocked me as she said, "I don't want to ever grow up and have to live with men. They are such beasts. All they want is a good-looking slave. There are probably no men who really respect women any more." While I reassured her that there are men who respect women and I pointed out the high value that Jesus placed on women, I have to confess to a haunting fear that there is more prejudice awaiting her than perhaps I was willing to admit. Attitudes toward men and women confuse many teens.

Vocational Choices

A sixth major problem facing today's youth results from the explosion of vocational options and the shifting world economic scene. Youth are not only faced with literally thousands of job alternatives, but they know that as the world economy shifts, there is no way to prepare for forty years or longer in the job market. Added to the perplexing maze of vocational decision making is the necessity for early educational decisions. Adolescents are pushed even in middle school to make vocational decisions and to begin to grow up vocationally. As David Elkind points out in his exciting volume *All Grown Up and No Place to Go,* today's adolescents receive too much pressure to succeed vocationally from the beginning.

Asian-American adolescents seem to be under even more pressure than their Hispanic, Black, and Anglo peers. Academic performance and vocational success, while obviously correlated, receive too much attention in many homes. Perhaps the greatest error is not to teach adolescents to understand their unique personalities as a gift from God. So often we fail to assist them in understanding the nature of Christian vocation and calling. The drive to get rich or to be famous overshadows responding to the call of God to service.

Matthew, a successful attorney's son, was ready to drop out of school his junior year of high school although he tested as above average in his academic ability and intelligence. His rebellion centered around a deep fear that no matter what he did, he could never please nor compete with his father. After several weeks of searching, Matthew was finally able to admit that he wanted to be in drama and he loved trucks. His dream was quite unsatisfactory in his father's mind. Matt still desired to drive trucks coast to coast and have time to perhaps pursue amateur filmmaking. Only after his father and mother began to bless his right to choose vocationally did he find any interest in performing to the level of his capability in school. Understandably, parents have dreams for their children's vocational success. But when those dreams become close-minded pressure on the part of the parents, teenagers experience vocational decision making as a nightmare. When the parents place too much emphasis on success and not enough on service, youth despair.

A host of other problems erupt regularly in adolescent society. Depression, suicide, automobile accidents, eating disorders, and brushes with the law all add to the fears of many parents. The ability to talk with teenagers, and not be shocked by the kinds of problems they are facing, will lay a foundation for pastors, parents, and other helping professionals to guide teens through the dangers of these crises toward opportunities for growth. Those who believe that God is at work in all things for good can indeed find hope in assisting adolescents to talk through whatever crisis they may be facing. The foundation of hope is at the heart of reaching out to touch the life of a bruised teenager.

Faith Crises

Perhaps the issue of greatest concern for many is the faith crises facing adolescents. A number of parents turn to me in alarm with statements like: "I don't know how to keep Sally interested in church," "Carlos doesn't seem to believe the things we have taught him any longer," and "Felton says he doesn't get anything from our pastor's preaching." "What can I do, what can I do, what can I do?" comes the avalanche of inquiries from fathers and mothers whose youth are turning away from the church. It can be expected that even teenagers who as children were given a good faith foundation will begin to question that foundation as adolescents. Their cognitive development gives them the capacity to see issues in a new way. Adolescents are ready for the meat of the faith; and when parents and churches continue to feed them on the milk of the faith that they received during childhood, they will rebel. Youth cast aside their childhood faith or compartmentalize faith into an area of life that is irrelevant for real decision making. The issue is not how do we keep them in their childhood faith, but how do we assist them to grow to new levels of spiritual wisdom and maturity? Even adolescents who make significant faith decisions as children may need to reconfirm those decisions as teenagers, and they will certainly need to think through their commitments from the new perspective of their increased intellectual abilities. Now that they can think abstractly and deal easily with ambiguities, youth should be expected to face new faith issues. Churches that provide the freedom for young persons to talk openly about their doubts and their faith issues can provide a much-needed ministry that will assist these same adolescents to mature spiritually.

Adolescents are capable of deep spiritual maturity and should be provided opportunities to engage in prayer and open Bible study in order to advance their spiritual development. While teens are frequently energized in more activity-oriented kinds of worship, worship leaders need to be careful not to exclude reflection, contemplation, and meditation from the worship opportunities of adolescents. Because youth are differentiating themselves from parental structures, they quite understandably will raise questions about power and authority in the church. When given opportunity to discuss these issues openly, they can develop a new sense of appreciation not only for the authority of God, but for the beauty of the church as the family of God. The goal is to assist them to no longer define the church as "they" but to see the power of God from within themselves and to begin to define the church as "us."

Hope in Face of Problems

Having surveyed briefly some of the problems confronting today's teens, let us now turn for a word of hope. There is promise for the future as the story of each teenager unfolds; our response can help them to write a new chapter. Few adults, parents included, are capable of drawing only on their own adolescent experience to provide understanding and hope for today's group of teens. Each new generation experiences the frustration of encountering teenagers who like themselves must learn through their own experiences. From the beginning of recorded history, adults have expressed considerable doubt and perhaps even anger toward the adolescent generation:

> I see no hope for the future of our people, if they are dependent upon the frivolous youth of today. For certainly all youth are reckless beyond words. When I was a boy, we were taught to be discreet and respectful of elders, but the present youth are exceedingly wild and inpatient of restraint.

These words come not from a frustrated parent of the 1990s but from Hesiod, and they were written in the eighth century B.C. (Group for the Advancement of Psychiatry, 7).

Talking About Possibilities

Just as universal as the lack of confidence in the adolescent generation is the diversity of issues that most professionals feel will provide hope to redeem the situation. Ask twenty youth counselors to make a list of the foundations for hope in assisting today's teenagers, and you will undoubtedly have twenty different lists. I invite you at this time to stop reading and make your own list of factors on which you feel the hope of the next generation rests. I also invite you to reflect on a tentative list that I provide.

Teens Need Adults Who Listen

If the next generation is indeed to benefit from the current generation's wisdom, we need to reverse the intended flow of information. Even the title of this book betrays that process. One youth suggested a book on "How to Listen to Your Teenager." Adult generations long for the opportunity to talk to youth so they will learn. In reality, youth values, commitments, and beliefs are more likely to be shaped by adults who are committed to listen, listen, and listen. Adults who know how to hear not only the story line of an adolescent's dialogue but also the complexities of feelings and unmet needs will have more influence in shaping that young person's future. Many adults have difficulty listening to teens because they can be so rebellious, obnoxious, loud, disrespectful, and even repulsive. Listening long enough to get through the teen's resistance rewards most adults with a genuine, honest look into the youth's life. Listening earns credibility and establishes a bridge between the teenager and the adult over which the adult can transmit information, attitudes, and values at a later time. The hope for tomorrow's adolescents is in an adult generation that knows how to listen.

Adolescents Need Time

A second ingredient in transforming the future of adolescents is time. While many parents bemoan the fact that they spend volumes of time in caring for their infant children, they speak with relieved joy because their teenagers can now take care of themselves. In many respects, youth need more time from their parents than do early school-age children. Perhaps they need almost as much time as infants. But the time is a different kind of time. They don't need controlled restriction; they need *enabling* time. Most parents do not know how to love an adolescent by giving them the gift of their time. Quality time between parents, teachers, ministers, and adolescents is an essential for productive interchange across generational lines. Youth need time to dream and someone to listen as they discuss those dreams in an environment of interest, acceptance, and then reality. Youth who spend time processing their dreams can do their reality testing of those dreams. They need someone to listen to their hopes more than they need a quality control expert to point out the limitations.

Teens need time to tell their stories to devoted adults that care about their lives and the personal details. Phrases like "Tell me more," "Anything else?" and "Explain that a bit further" not only communicate a desire to know their world, but also a willingness to spend the time to do so.

Teenagers Need Freedom

Adolescents need freedom. They need the freedom to explore, at least verbally, a variety of alternatives for every decision that they make. They need the freedom, within limits, to talk about their doubts, their dreams, and their frustrations. They need the freedom to walk through decisions and role-play situations. They deserve the freedom to choose for themselves as often as possible.

Teens Need to Make Decisions

Adults should not make decisions for teenagers when they are capable of making those decisions for themselves. Adolescents should make decisions, for example, about the kinds of clothes they wear as long as the clothing is not unhealthy for them. Adolescents can also participate in family decision making. They deserve the freedom to explore at least in conversation the likely consequences of a variety of family decisions.

Young People Need Limits

While a number of parents react in fear and hold on tightly to their teens, there is also a group, perhaps even larger, who let go too soon and refuse to assist their adolescents in understanding limits and setting limits on life. Restricting a young person's freedom is often a misdirected love. Giving adolescents too much freedom is often an expression of unconcern and a lack of love. Some parents are so preoccupied with their own problems, addictions, and mixed-up behavior that they cannot or will not assist in setting limits for their teenagers. Other parents, out of a misunderstanding of the meaning of freedom, fail to provide adequate limits and guidance for their youth. One of the first methods of treatment for adolescents who are institutionalized in substance abuse and psychiatric centers is a firm set of limits with clear guidelines as to how freedom is earned. Most youth respond positively and find security within the limits. The hope for tomorrow's teenagers rests with adults who know how to say no and set appropriate, realistic limits for adolescents. Generally speaking, the limits are tighter in early adolescence and are loosened as the teenager demonstrates responsibility and wisdom in making decisions. If the teen becomes irresponsible in the face of too much freedom, limits need to be reassessed and perhaps tightened. Open, clear communication between adults and teenagers is necessary for this process of tightening and loosening of limits to be effective.

Adolescents Need Family Stability

A further need for adolescents is for family stability and structure. Adolescents need to know that no matter what happens, their family structure is intact. This does not so much mean that the nuclear family will hold together, but it means that there are significant adults (perhaps biologically related, perhaps not) who are willing to say, "No matter what happens to you, I still care. You can always turn to me for help." Such stability provides the young person a network of support in which to work out significant struggles.

The structure and stability of the family unit also takes into account family expectations and rules. Each group of persons has its spoken and unspoken guidelines for acceptable and unacceptable behavior. Adolescents need to know that the rules are fair, meaningful, and flexible. For the rules to be fair, teenagers need to feel that they and the adults live by the same rules. For example, if there is a family rule of no name-calling or disrespectful yelling, the parent and adult figures should expect to treat the youth in the same manner.

For rules to be meaningful, they have to apply to life as it really is. Some family rules were meant for a period of time several generations back. When rules are not updated and in step with the times, adolescents will not feel the security of a stable family structure. They will know their family is irrelevant. For example, one father had set a rule that in their household they always helped the women on with their sweaters and coats. In his words, it was the "gentlemanly thing to do." When his sixteen-year-old son had stopped by the house with a date for a few hours, the father chided him for not helping the young lady on with her coat as they were leaving. Later the son explained to him that this particular sixteen-year-old girl felt it was an insult to have a date help her on with her sweater. She felt that women and men as equals could care for themselves. A number of such social rules change with the passing of time. Families must be flexible enough to update or at least renegotiate their rules and communicate openly about them in order for the teens to feel the rules are meaningful.

Flexibility of rules seems self-evident. While some rules are enduring and obviously universal ("Thou shalt not kill"), other rules need to be negotiable, like the previous illustration. Effective communication with adolescents demands that at least the guidelines are up for discussion and negotiation. Parents who must depend on retorts like, "Because I say so," and, "That's the way it is in this family," stifle the hope for open communication with adolescents in the future.

Youth Need Dependable Relationships with Adults

The promise for young persons in the future depends also on dependable relationships with adults. Adults who live consistently with their values engender trust in the youth around them. Teenagers who can trust their adult world are more likely to negotiate creative, growth-producing pathways through their adjustment years.

More than a few adults complain that they cannot trust adolescents. My experience has been mistrust is most often taught by some adult in their lives. An adult who has betrayed them has modeled untrustworthy behavior for the teens. Such modeling drowns out any lecture or teaching to the contrary. Adolescents who experience the unfaithfulness of adults develop deep patterns of mistrust. Of course, it would be expected that these patterns did not begin in the teen years, but the unfaithfulness and the lack of bonding in the relationship goes far back into childhood. Indeed, if there is to be hope for adolescents, it must be built on mutual trust between them and the adults in their world.

Likewise, affirmation is central to growth-producing relationships between adolescents and the adults in their immediate and larger family. Surprisingly, many families become embarrassed at the giving and receiving of honest affirmation. In fact, some substitute harsh criticism and witty sarcasm for affirmation. When families lack the capacity to honestly say, "I appreciate a given behavior," they greatly limit the capacities for communication in other areas. To be able to give and receive a compliment is at the heart of healthy family relationships. A part of the promise for future generations is that adolescents are taught to express praise and gratitude to others in their world and to receive it graciously from them.

Teenagers Need a Meaningful Faith Experience

The ultimate foundation for hope of the future of adolescents is a meaningful faith experience. The spiritual dimension of a youth's life is *the* element that integrates all others. Adolescents need a spiritual mentor or guide who not only knows how to creatively get their attention, perhaps through games or recreation, but also knows how to honestly search with them, introduce them to faith issues, and nurture them along the pilgrimage toward spiritual maturity.

Having discussed the problems and promises for the future in the adolescent world, we now turn our attention to another story. Remember, these stories are shared for your use in reaching out to teenagers. You may wish to discuss all or some of these stories with your teenager or youth group and use the questions in the "For You-th Discussion" section.

Lonely Stories

Trish, a lonely, depressed, freckle-faced bundle of pain, attempted to take her own life by overdosing on a bottle of her grandmother's pills. Fortunately, she called to say good-bye and passed out while on the phone. I called the Emergency Medical Services and met her at the hospital. When she was able to talk, Trish revealed that she felt no one cared for her. She couldn't stand feeling so alone.

As Trish returned from the hospital, adults in her family chided her for trying to kill herself. She began crying. A five-year-old niece crawled into her lap and muttered a healing message: "Trish," she said, looking up with her big brown eyes, "I don't care what you have done. I still love you." Trish's loneliness was overcome with the joy of one person who loved her unconditionally. The Bible says, "A little child shall lead them" (Isa. 11:6, KJV). Unless we become as little children we will not know the kingdom of heaven. I believe that the little niece revealed a portion of the kingdom of heaven that day.

Trish, like many youth, had experienced isolation and loneliness, but it was overcome with the straightforward declaration of love.

You may feel lonely as you read this. It's possible to experience loneliness in a crowd. Loneliness hurts, doesn't it? Loneliness is a state of being, a feeling, a thought that you belong with, to, or around no one. It's the belief that no one belongs with, to, or around you—at least no one that matters. Loneliness is feeling no one really cares.

David experienced loneliness on a retreat with thirty-seven other youth. I observed that when they played, he just watched. When the group was singing, he would just listen. As they worked on projects, he stood to one side. When they began to share deeply, he left. I saw David walking off by himself and followed him toward the lake.

"What's the matter, David?" I inquired as I began to walk at his side. "You look like you've lost your last friend. Want to talk?" I asked when he didn't respond to my first inquiry.

"What difference does it make?" he finally blurted out.

"Who is 'it'?" I prodded.

"I am it!" he yelled. "What difference do I make? I mean these people don't give me the time of day. Have you noticed they don't care if I'm around here or not? They don't care about me one bit."

"Maybe they don't, David. I suspect they are just too busy trying not to be lonely themselves, but I can't defend them. At least, I can say I care about you. I may not be much, but I'm willing to listen."

David and I initiated a friendship on that retreat. He took the biggest risk. He began to let me care for him. As his loneliness ebbed away, he trusted the group. In a few days, I observed his participation with the others. Suddenly, there were thirty-eight youth on that retreat. David was playing, working, singing, and sharing with the group. He had found a very special gift—spiritual community. He thought, and rightly so, that they cared about him. He began to care about them.

I'm not sure when but at some point in our conversations several months later, I became aware that David was beginning to care about himself. The worst kind of loneliness is not being your own friend. The Bible tells us that we are to love our neighbor as *ourselves* (Matt. 22:39). When we can't love ourselves, we are cut off from the capacity to accept love from others. Youth who can't love themselves feel un-worthy of friends, undeserving of praise, unfit for fellowship, unfin-ished as a self, and unwanted as they are. The most painful loneliness results from being cut off from oneself. David simply didn't like him-self; but, as he began to let others into his life, he learned that he could like himself. A part of liking himself was the commitment to give him-self to help the group. David could sing quite well. The youth minister encouraged him to join the youth choir. After much inviting on the part of several of his peers, David finally attended one rehearsal. He was surprised to be affirmed for his ability and continued to partici-pate on a semiregular basis. Finding one activity in which to invest himself was a major turning point in learning to like himself.

Loneliness can be the result of losing a best friend. When friends move away, you naturally experience loneliness. When someone with whom you belong is gone, loneliness is understandable. When your family moves, massive loneliness results from a loss of all friends—those you cared about and those who cared about you are suddenly gone. The resulting grief often feels unbearable. When tragedy strikes and someone you love dies, the grief can be even more intense.

Cindy was fourteen when her father and mother moved eight hun-dred miles to Oklahoma City. She lost her five best friends. In the same month, Cindy's big sister went away to college. Cindy and her parents lived alone. For the first six months in the new community, Cindy begged her parents to move back. She felt that seeing her friends back home was the only solution to her loneliness. However, she gradually made friends in her new school, church, and neighbor-hood. At first, it was natural for her to compare these new friends to the old ones, and, of course, the new friends didn't begin to measure up. There was something wrong with everyone of them. Cindy knew they were creeps, but they were all she had. She could hardly wait until summer vacation. Her parents had promised she could return for two weeks to visit her old friends. To her surprise, they didn't seem as great as she had remembered them. Her grief and loneliness had blocked their faults out of her memory and caused her to overly ro-manticize their good points. After the two weeks when she returned to her new home, Cindy was surprised that she was really glad to see those new friends. She thought she even belonged there now. She soon forgot about being lonely.

For You-th Discussion

What makes you lonely? When were you last lonely? Are you lonely now? What can you do about loneliness? In the jean-age generation, there are some definite alternatives to suffering through loneliness all alone. Admitting loneliness is the first step to recovery. Accept the fact that you hurt. Tell someone that you feel alone. Own your loneliness, claim it. Know that it's yours. Then think hopefully. Where can you ask for help? What are your alternatives? Who might care about you? Even if they aren't the best, who might care? Your little brother or sister? The nerd next door? The friend that you would never date? Who does care about you? Your idol, that teacher at school? Make a list of people who might care just a little bit. Make a list of adults that you can begin to trust—people who know the jean-age generation— and then go talk to them about your loneliness. Maybe your list would include a courageous teacher, a caring minister, a courteous neighbor, or a compassionate youth. As you talk with them, promise to move out of your silence and solitude. The dialogue will start you on a self-discovery process; it might even help you to like yourself and be liked by the other person. Taking a risk to let others know who you are can be a big step in overcoming loneliness.

Learn to listen to yourself—that's right, I said listen to yourself. Youth who can dialogue with their inner voice have someone with whom to talk. Be still, turn off the noise in your room. Unplug the TV, turn off the radio, shut down the stereo, take off the headphones, find a quiet place, and listen to you. Listen to your head. What are you thinking? What's that thought leaning toward? Listen to your heart. Ask yourself how do you feel about those thoughts running through your mind? Do you think someone has cheated you, and you feel angry? Do you think someone has exposed you, and you feel embarrassed? Do you think someone has broken a promise, and you feel disappointed? Or perhaps you think you've made a mistake, and you feel guilty. Whatever you feel—sad, bad, mad, or glad—get to know yourself and decide to tell someone about that feeling. Reaching out with your feelings combats loneliness.

Now look around. There are probably teenagers more lonely than you. You might retort, "There's no one lonelier than I am." Perhaps that's true, but I doubt it. You don't know other persons' loneliness because they're hiding it just like you used to. And in your loneliness you haven't been seeking them out; admit it. You haven't noticed them. There are lonely youth all around you. Look over by the wall at the party. Look at the chairs outside the circle in your discussion group. Look at those who never get in the game during activities. You won't notice them unless you look. Use your own loneliness as a pair of glasses to see their loneliness. Then take a risk: walk over to them and help them get involved. Along the path toward them, you'll lose your loneliness.

One final reflection for you jean-agers on loneliness: let God into your loneliness. God is like a light shining into the darkness of loneliness. God is love overcoming the hatred of loneliness. He is reality pushing aside the pretension of loneliness. God is awareness easing the numbness of loneliness. He is aliveness awakening the stillness of loneliness. God is dependability destroying the uncertainty of loneliness. Remember, the God who watches over the sparrows of the sky has promised to watch over even you. God is your friend (Matt. 10:26-33). God travels with those who journey through the jean-age years. Awakening one's life to the presence of God is the ultimate overcoming of loneliness.

2

The Art of Storytelling
with Teenagers

Storytelling suggests various meanings for most of us. One of the first thoughts that pops into our minds may be of people not telling the truth. Sometimes little white lies are referred to as telling a story as opposed to telling the truth. This is not the context in which this book uses storytelling. Storytelling means rather "the sharing of a sequence of events that conveys meaning beyond just the events themselves." Storytelling can mean just the art of entertaining others, but it is used here to go beyond entertaining in order to convey a deeper message. "I Love to tell the story / Because I know 'tis true"; "We've a story to tell to the nations"; "Tell Me the Story of Jesus"—each of these hymn lines refers to the story! The small, rural church of my youth spoke boldly of *the* story. As we communicate through stories to teenagers, ultimately the story of Christ Jesus is the message we hope to communicate. There are many aspects of the gospel story, many implications of understanding how that story impels us to live a life of love in service to others. Jesus, undoubtedly the greatest storyteller ever, frequently communicated His message through parables and stories of every-day life. More importantly, the story of His life communicates the revelation of God to all persons in all times.

The Telling

The art of storytelling with teenagers can be learned; one's storytelling skills can be developed. Granted, some persons are more naturally storytellers than others. Certain personality types communicate through symbol and story while others long for the cold hard facts and give-me-the-bottom-line communication. Even if you, the reader, already communicate fairly well through stories, perhaps a few how-to guidelines will strengthen your storytelling with teenagers. Ask for regular feedback from other adults and teenagers whom you trust as you polish your storytelling techniques. Here are a few reflections on how to tell a story to teenagers that I have found helpful.

Know the Audience

Knowing one's audience is a time-tested axiom of public communication. This is certainly true with storytelling with teens. One needs to know teenagers in general and the specific context of the teenagers being addressed. Stories that communicate with teenagers in the inner city may not communicate with youth in a small-town midwestern community, in the mountains of Appalachia, in the sprawling suburbs of the West Coast, in the pure air of a Rocky Mountain ski community, in the heat of a beach community, or in the Deep South. Effective stories contain elements of the culture that are readily known and reflect processes that are understandable. For example, inner-city adolescents may have difficulty identifying with agricultural stories. Likewise, farming-community youth may not understand a story about streetwise behavior in an inner-city ghetto. Ghetto youth may not understand a popular humorous story from Appalachia (Why did the chicken cross the road? To show a "possum" it could be done). It takes a unique storyteller, in fact, to tell stories that cut across adolescents' cultural limitations. While there are undoubtedly universal themes, the particulars of the story may need to be modified in order to meet the audience as you know it.

Knowing the family context is also important. To know that a particular group of youth are predominantly without fathers in the home can be important information before retelling the story of the prodigal son. To know the favorite sport or the kind of music appreciated by a particular subgroup of teenagers enhances one's ability to communicate through story. Knowing the particular stories of a given group of teenagers and tying the story into some of those elements can further increase the effectiveness of communication. For example, knowing that a small community has suffered a crisis resulting in the tragic death of two adolescents can be significant information in telling a story where grief is involved.

Keep the Stories Authentic

While modifying one's story elements and images in light of the given cultural context may be important, one must be certain that the stories are authentic and that the storyteller comes across as "real" to the youth. Adolescents can spot a put-on, a phony, or a false prophet more quickly than any other age group. Clear, honest, appropriate communication must be at the center of storytelling with youth. The integrity of the storyteller relates not only through the story but through the rest of the storyteller's relationships to the group. In short, the group must respect the storyteller. While some respect can be ascribed to the storyteller by other adults whom the youth trust, ultimately respect must be earned even in a short period of time by the storyteller's authentic relationships with the youth.

Use Active Stories

Youth respond to vigorous, alive stories with movement. Cars don't drive down a racetrack, they roar down the homestretch. Flowers don't just bloom, they burst into color. Thunder isn't just heard, it explodes. Ideas don't just come to the mind, they rush to the mind. For technical assistance in communicating with activity and aliveness, see the book *Words on Target* by Sue Nichols.

Keep the Stories Subtle

Teenagers seem to respond to stories that kind of sneak up on them rather than present the message in too obvious a way. While communication needs to be clear and direct, effective stories have a subtle and mysterious side that lures the teenager into involvement. Effective stories with teenagers assist them in losing themselves in the story. Undoubtedly, we have all had the experience of being so caught up in reading the description of a snowstorm that when we turn from our book we are surprised to see that there's no snow in our real world. Good storytellers know how to keep the audience spellbound. The subtle nature of the story does not mean the story is to be unclear, nondescriptive, and without color. Many times storytellers ruin the message for adolescents by backing up and explaining it to them several times after the story has been told. Avoid the temptation to over-tell the point of your story. Permit the adolescents to ask questions afterwards or to dialogue with each other, but do not insult their intelligence through oversimplification.

Use Adventure and Excitement

Adolescents seem attracted to stories with adventure, excitement, surprise, movement, color, and mystery. They like stories that deal with themes from their own world struggles. The success of the *Star Wars, Back to the Future,* and *Star Trek* movie series should tell us volumes about adolescent storytelling. Some movie makers have decided to particularly target their stories with adolescent themes in mind. Movies like *Ferris Buehler's Day Off, Sixteen Candles, The Breakfast Club,* and *Look Who's Talking* all appeal directly to adolescent themes—themes like rebellion against authority, clever teen trickery defeats the adult system, and the personal pain of forgotten individuals. These themes attract adolescents like moths to a flame, bees to nectar, and mosquitos to a campfire devotional.

The Timing

The art of storytelling with teenagers not only involves understanding *how* to tell stories, but it's important to know *when* to tell stories. The timing of a story is more than knowing how to utilize silence, rate of speech, and development of the plot. The timing of the story can also be in knowing when, in the development of a relationship, a story will communicate. Just as there is a time to speak and a time to keep silent in one-to-one communication, there's a time to tell stories and a time to refrain from telling stories in public communication. Not all sermon settings are conducive to storytelling, but when a number of teenagers are expected to be in the congregation, or when speaking to an entire congregation of youth, storytelling needs to be considered as an effective alternative to traditional forms of sermonizing. Certainly devotionals and retreat messages can be effective times for storytelling. I have observed effective storytellers like the late Grady Nutt tell a story that the audience assumed would introduce a message and wind up twenty minutes later having captivated the audience in such a way that the story communicated the message, but only at the end.

Use Stories in Bible Study

As an eleventh-grade Sunday School teacher, I frequently use stories throughout various parts of the Sunday School lesson. Obviously, stories can be an effective means of preparing for the lesson, but sometimes retelling a Bible story can be an effective way of teaching the lesson. Certainly, sharing stories such as case studies can significantly contribute to the application section of the lesson. Students are frequently brought into participation by the request to tell their stories around a given topic. For example, students were recently asked to communicate a time when they had made a sacrifice that turned out to be a "cup of cold water in Jesus' name." As they took turns telling a time they had given something meaningful to another, a sense of the presence of God enveloped the classroom, and the students became aware that God was indeed speaking through them.

Use Stories in Counseling

Individual counseling and group counseling with youth can be enriched through well-selected, properly timed, creatively shared stories. I recall an incident when a young man in depression felt the pain of rejection from a group of peers at his church. As I attempted to lead him in sharing his hurt, a wall of resistance stood between us. After asking if I could share a brief story and receiving a shrug and an "I guess so," I took a risk to briefly tell of another young man who had been bussed from a small rural school into a consolidated high school. A few humorous incidents around this "country bumpkin's" attempts to fit in soon had the youth smiling and even chuckling under his breath. When at the end of the story I revealed I was that misfit, his look of surprise invited further conversation. Although not disarmed, the youth's resistance did lower enough that we could continue to build a relationship. He could believe that perhaps others understood his embarrassment and shame. Storytelling in individual counseling builds rapport and establishes a bridge of relationship over which effective help can be transported.

Storytelling in group counseling, likewise a means of establishing trust, can more often be a way of involving the group in sharing with each other. Just as beginning Sunday School teachers sometimes make the error of having all the communication between teacher and students, some group counseling with teenagers becomes too leader oriented. Effective facilitators of group dynamics know how to use stories to assist the youth to speak to each other as well as to the leader. Common stories known to all of the group or even songs popular in the youth culture can be shared briefly. Request that group members share with one another what they think the story means, at what points they identify with the story, or even how they think the story should be changed.

The Touch

Knowing when and how to tell stories facilitates the art of storytelling with adolescents, but one must never forget why the stories are told. Ultimately, the stories are to communicate the nature of God and the nature of human interaction to the adolescent. Healing the teen's relationship to God, self, and others remains our ultimate purpose. Stories must have the touch that promotes wholeness. Touch is the why of storytelling.

To Bridge Understanding

Sometimes we tell stories to build a bridge of understanding between ourselves and the adolescents. We want them to believe that we can know them and their world. We want them to know we can understand them. Reciprocally, we want teens to know that we are willing to be understood; we are willing to be vulnerable, take risks, and expose who we are through our stories. Sometimes we tell stories to assist teenagers to put labels on their own experiences. They hear the story and hopefully respond, "Ah ha! That's what it's like for me!" They hear a feeling word and claim it as their own. For example, they might say, "Yes, I felt lost like the prodigal son." Or, "I know how Joseph's brothers must have felt with his getting all the special attention from the parents." Stories that help adolescents identify and communicate their own feelings and emotions touch their hearts.

To Speak the Unspeakable

Stories assist teens to speak the unspeakable. Their own shame, pain, embarrassment, and hurt are frequently so intense that only through stories and parables can adolescents communicate what has happened to them. Often such stories are shared first through writing. I recall having an adolescent read a story about a mother who abandoned her children, and then he wrote his response. I knew his own mother was an alcoholic currently serving time in a state prison. He could not discuss the story in a group context, but he did write a rather extensive response story, telling of his own longing to be loved by his mother and to find someone he could love.

To Assess Adolescents' Life Situation

Projective stories are sometimes used as a part of assessing an adolescent's world view, moral values, feeling tones, or general situation in life. While stories can be effective tools in discovering an adolescent's condition, one must be careful not to rely on them solely. Getting a cross-reference from other professionals, perhaps from testing, and from personal conversation, strengthens the assessment that comes through storytelling.

To Educate

Obviously, another "why" for telling stories is for education. Youth frequently remember a story and the truth it conveys more than they remember abstract truth. Stories are the containers that carry truth from generation to generation. The art of storytelling is significantly enhanced if we know how, when, and why we are telling the stories. Let us turn our attention to a number of types of stories.

Just as an artist uniquely selects the materials for a sculpture, one must carefully select the content of a story. Just as a sculptor does not want the grain of the wood to detract from his carving, a storyteller does not want the elements of the story to detract from its own ultimate meaning. A unique cedar carving of nativity figures uses the change of the color of the wood fiber to creatively distinguish the robes and garments of the figures. Likewise, a skilled storyteller uses the elements of the story to all point to the totality of the message. No one element should be so attractive as to detract from the story. Any of these types may be used in any context.

The Types

In reality, the types frequently overlap, but for the sake of understanding, they will be isolated and illustrated separately. One story may have several levels of meaning and actually serve different purposes for different adolescents in the same group. For example, a story that assists in teaching a lesson to one member of the group might be building rapport with another and eliciting further involvement from still another youth. There are many different types of stories and a variety of plots that develop. However, this typology evolves from the focus of the stories.

Bible Stories

Bible stories comprise the largest percentage of stories shared by religious workers with teenagers. The focus of teaching the Scripture certainly accounts for the volume of these stories. Nevertheless, many times teens seem to desire the ancient stories of the Bible. Serious Bible study appeals to a large number of well-disciplined, spiritually alive adolescents. Too frequently, youth ministers err on the side of under-challenging some adolescents with the meat of the Scripture.

Repetition can be boring for teenagers who were reared in regular Bible study. One youth complained, "If I hear one more story about David and Goliath, I think I'll throw up." It seems that the overdependence of some religious education curriculum on the same stories has its negative side for youth who have been involved in religious studies over the long term. However, adolescents who are new in the faith may find these stories refreshing and exciting.

Youth seem particularly mesmerized by dramatized biblical stories. More than a few ministers have been effective in dressing in biblical garb and retelling stories that vary from Paul's missionary journeys to observations and reflections from the point of view of Judas Iscariot.

Adolescents like the dramatization because it helps them visualize and identify with what otherwise might be only an abstract image or idea. Other ministers have found monologue sermons difficult with adolescents, particularly if the teenagers have a very limited understanding of the Scripture. It seems that the monologue sermons are best received by scripturally literate, not scripturally uninformed, teens.

Setting a biblical story in a contemporary context is another successful approach with youth and was one hallmark of minister and entertainer Grady Nutt. His retelling of the story of the prodigal son helped teenagers to identify with the rebellious youth as well as his jealous brother. While the truth of the story can be well preserved as it is set in a contemporary context, one must be careful not to take too much liberty in retelling such biblical stories.

> There was a middle-aged dude who had two sons. The younger of the two, being fairly restless, said to him one day, "Hey, Pop, some day you're going to die, and all that you have is going to be half mine. How about giving me my half now?" The father did it. He liquidated his assets and gave the boy his half. Not wanting to look too obvious, the kid stuck around for several days. But then one day he packed his bags, jumped in the sports car he had bought with part of his father's inheritance, and split to southern California where he began living in the fast lane. He partied and squandered what he had for some time.
>
> Just as his tough luck would have it, a recession hit about the time he was running short of bread. So he had to take a menial job cleaning stables at a racetrack. He had to clean the stalls and feed the livestock. He wasn't paid much, lost his apartment, and began sleeping with the animals. In fact, he wound up eating with the animals. He was dirty, filthy, and hungry.
>
> One day he came to his senses and said, "My dad's lowest-paid workers have enough to eat, and I'm here starving to death. I'm going to hitchhike back home, tell the old man that I made a big mistake, and see if he won't give me a job. I know I'm not worthy to be called his son, but maybe he'll at least give me a decent job."
>
> Rides didn't come easy—it took him some time to get back into his home state. As he was walking down his street, he saw his dad on the front porch. To his surprise, his dad ran down the steps, down the street, grabbed him, and began dancing up and down, hugging him, and

really made a scene. As soon as the boy could quiet him down he said, "Dad, Dad, wait a minute. I've made a big mistake. I'm really not worthy to be called your son." But the father called to some of his employees and said, "Quickly, get some of my better clothes, help him get cleaned up, put those clothes on him, and give him the credit card and a checkbook. We're going to have a feast. Go down to the store and buy some of the best steaks you can find. As a matter of fact, let's cater a party tonight. This boy was as good as lost, but now he's home."

About half way through the party, the older brother drove into the driveway. He had worked late at the family business—again. He heard the music and laughter and was puzzled. He asked one of his dad's employees, "What in the world is going on?" The man said, "You won't believe it. Your brother came home, and your father has gone crazy over him. He's having a big party." The older brother was really ticked off. He said, "I'm not going in. I can't believe he's done this." Just then the father came out on the porch and saw him. In exuberant joy the father began to chatter, "Your brother has come home. I'm so glad to see him!" The older brother began to complain. "You mean to tell me that after all these years that I've worked for you, you can party when that bum comes back home? You've never given me a party in all the time I've been with you. If that doesn't beat everything." The father said to him, "Listen, son, you've always been with me, and you know that everything I have is going to be yours. It is fitting now that we celebrate your brother coming home. He was as good as dead, and now he is alive. I thought he was lost for good, but he's back."

When Jesus first told this story, He was telling it to two groups. The Pharisees and scribes had been murmuring because Jesus had been talking with and eating with sinners, and the sinners themselves no doubt overheard this story. The message was clear. The sinners were the younger brother, and they had hope because they had just returned. But the scribes and Pharisees, here pictured as the older brother, were in danger of losing the relationship to the father because they failed to exhibit grace to those who were lost.

Extensive biblical research can assist in a third approach to telling biblical stories. A prominent biblical scholar suggests that Scripture be placed in its emotional context with attention drawn to all of the bodily senses in order to bring the story to life and to put the listener in the midst of the story. (See Walter Wink, *Transforming Bible Study*.) For example, in telling the story of Jesus' encounter with the woman at the well, the storyteller might ask listeners to imagine being in the desert on a blistering hot day at high noon. They could feel the burning of the hot wind on their faces, imagine their parched mouths, smell the dry, dusty air, and feel the cool water as it was drawn from the well. They might hear the footsteps crunching in the sand as someone approached from behind, taste the dust as it blew up from His shoes, and see the kindness in the face of Jesus. They might feel the fear, the shame, of the woman at the well being discovered for who she really was. As the storyteller draws the listeners into the context, the power of Jesus' words strikes a more personal chord for the listener.

Transformational Stories

A number of stories fall into a second category, which I choose to call transformational stories. Transformational stories are designed to assist adolescents in finding an authentic self through stories that call them to journey toward wholeness. Although there are numerous transformational stories, we will consider just four: hero stories, inspirational stories, other culture stories, and ethical twist stories.

Hero Stories.—Because of selected reading, many of the hero stories retold from the Bible are male hero figures. There are a number, however, of heroines in both the Old and New Testaments: Ruth, Esther, Mary, and Priscilla are but a few.

Hero stories are an obvious opportunity for adolescents to project themselves into the hero role. As they identify with the heroes in the story, they can call their values, attitudes, and beliefs into question and imagine themselves being a hero. Hero stories serve to reinforce positive identity formation among youth. It is particularly useful for adolescents when the biblical hero is a young person, such as Joseph, David, Timothy, Titus, or Esther.

Some teens have such a negative self-image and a distorted value system that they might see the heroes in the role of a fool. One teenager responded to the story of the lad who gave his lunch to Jesus for the feeding of the five thousand, "There ain't no way that kid's going to be dumb enough to give up his own lunch. Why he'd take that behind some rock and eat it if he was smart!" This young man's response to the story betrays not only his own lack of compassion, but it points as well to perhaps a history of abuse that has hardened him to the point of always looking out for number one.

As one retells the hero stories of people like Esther, it is important to point out the persons' probable age during the time of the story. Adolescents identify more easily once they know that Esther was most likely less than twenty years old. Be cautious in sharing stories like Esther's that the cultural dimensions, such as being given by one's father in marriage or perhaps polygamy, do not completely overshadow the deeper message of faithfulness, commitment, and devotion.

Inspirational Stories.—These stories certainly abound in Scripture, but a variety of stories exist in classic literature as well as in contemporary writings. Inspirational stories are designed to help youth reach for the stars. These stories facilitate the development of teenagers' potential and inspire them toward commitment. Inspirational stories can be particularly helpful as youth are preparing for mission projects, special musical presentations, and other forms of service to the church, school, or community. If one is going to use the more traditional hero stories of Scripture like the young David going into battle against the giant Goliath, it is perhaps best to update the story as was done with the story of the prodigal son. However, less popular biblical stories can be shared effectively in their original context, as would be the case with the story of Ruth and her commitment to Naomi.

There are many inspirational stories from literature that inspire youth to sacrificial giving. For instance, two young lovers are so poor that they cannot afford a gift for each other at the first Christmas after their marriage. Her long, beautiful hair—a source of pride for her—is cut off and sold in order to purchase a chain for his pocket watch. He, however, has sold his pocket watch in order to buy her bands for her hair. The sacrificial giving of each inspires teenagers to understand the deeper levels of mature love necessary for a romantic relationship to develop into a long-term, meaningful marriage.

More contemporary inspirational stories can arise from current events or case studies of adolescents in the community. For example, the story of an adolescent risking his or her life to swim out and rescue a child at the beach can be quite inspirational to a group of teens. I have frequently used the true case of a fifteen-year-old farm boy whose hand was caught in a piece of farm equipment and mangled so badly that the extensive surgery would take months to repair the muscles and tendons. During the long process of recovery and reconstruction, the young man became depressed. Only after his girlfriend traveled forty miles to visit with him and actually hold the mangled hand did he find new courage to continue to fight in the recovery process. Her willingness to touch his scar, to touch his mashed and mangled fingers, has inspired other youth to see beyond the shallowness of boyfriend/girlfriend relationships into selfless giving.

Other Culture's Stories.—Stories from other cultures not only inform but often confront teenagers as well. Adolescents are usually interested in customs of youth in other countries. Perhaps they are most interested in dating customs and customs in relating to parents, but transportation, food, schooling, and other common features of the adolescent world also capture their attention. A group of teens were surprised recently to learn that in portions of the Far East it is still not unusual for parents to prearrange the marriage of their children. As a young couple from India told the story of how his father had arranged for their marriage through her brother, the teenagers inquisitively asked about how their relationship then developed. "How does one learn to love someone after they're married?" asked one teenage girl. Shockingly, the response came, "Love may never come. But if it does, it is a gift of God." Stories of the long hours of study and the difficulty of getting into school in the Oriental culture have served to confront a number of American adolescents who take their educational opportunities for granted and reflect a casual attitude toward studies. (In a recent trip to Korea, I learned that the teenage girl in the home of the minister I was visiting spent ten hours each day during school vacation studying at the library for entrance exams.)

Ethical Twist Stories.—A fourth type of transformational story, ethical twist, is designed to lead youth to examine their decisions and the process of making choices. Leading youth to reflect upon their behavior is a difficult task; getting them to make decisions in an ethically consistent manner seems almost impossible. Stories offer hope.

While many teens will remember David's sin with Bathsheba—the story of how he looked down from his own rooftop to see her bathing, sent her husband into battle where he was sure to be killed, and then married her himself—they may not know the story of the confrontation. The prophet Nathan came to David and told the story of a man who had many sheep, and his neighbor had only one. When it came time for a feast, he sent to his neighbor and demanded his one sheep and killed it for the feast. The prophet asked the king what should be done. "Surely he should be severely punished," replied King David. "Thou art the man," said Nathan as he pointed his finger at David. Ethical confrontation stories can be used in a similar manner with adolescents. Selfishness can be confronted with the selfsame story.

Frequently, I have used a role reversal to help adolescents see the inconsistency in their values. I tell a story about two teens shopping in a large discount department store. As the first one is checking out to pay for a cassette tape of their latest rock idol, the second one notices that the friend has been shortchanged a dollar. The listeners are then asked what the friend should do. Ignore it, go back and ask for the dollar himself at a later time, or point it out and ask the clerk to give the friend the dollar. Almost universally, the teenagers say they would point out the error so that their friend could receive the proper change. Then I tell the story of checking out with the same friend, and the store is shortchanged a dollar. When I present them with the same alternatives, few teenagers decide to tell the clerk that the store is being cheated by a dollar. As we begin discussing the inconsistencies of the values reflected in the responses to the story, someone usually says that the big store won't miss it, implying that competitiveness—not right or wrong—is at the heart of making their decision.

Participation Stories

A third type of story used frequently with adolescents is participation story. These are stories that one way or another call for teenagers to share in the experience of the story. Each has its unique contribution to the art of talking with teenagers so they will listen. I invite you to consider the use of unfinished stories, committee-told stories, take-your-pick stories, and role plays.

Unfinished Stories.—A direct approach to drawing out adolescents, unfinished stories give them an opportunity to reveal parts of themselves otherwise unobservable. The process is simple: someone reads or tells a story in detail, but the ending is open-ended and incomplete. In working with a group of adolescents I find it's best to ask each person to write his or her version of the story's ending and then share it with the larger group. This minimizes group influence early in the process. When working with individuals, I usually permit them to verbalize how they would end the story. If they resist with something like, "I don't know," or, "I was never very good at stuff like this," I usually wait in silence for several minutes before even mentioning some alternatives. Frequently, with particularly difficult adolescents, I will tell them how one or two other teenagers ended the story and then ask them to pick the best from those choices or to modify and come up with their own ending.

"The Lady and the Tiger" is a classic unfinished story that has appealed to teenagers for generations. The story is set in medieval European times. A young man who is in love with the princess has been found out by her father and is placed in the arena to do battle. There are two doors: behind one is a tiger; behind the other, a lady. If he chooses the door with the tiger, he will surely die. If he opens the door with the lady, he can marry her but will never be able to see the princess again. As the young man bows before the king and his family, the princess indicates one of the doors. He strides across the arena to open the door, and as he does the story ends. Youth are to select the lady or the tiger. Which would the princess want for her love? You decide.

Several biblical stories are unfinished to a point. On occasion I have told the story of the good Samaritan and asked teenagers what they imagined happened when the good Samaritan finally arrived at his destination. How was he received by those who were expecting him to arrive several days earlier? What would they say? And why? Some teenagers have him encounter understanding persons who celebrate his deed of kindness. Others have him confront unsympathetic persons who don't want to hear his excuses for why he has failed to arrive on time. More than one teenager has him arriving to his family who are hurt and disappointed that he has not been with them.

A contemporary version of the unfinished story can be found in Shel Silverstein's "It and the Missing Piece." The story has a pac-manlike figure trying to find the piece that completes It as a circle. Without the piece, It confronts many situations in life: rain, snow, heat, and normal difficulties of traveling. As It searches for a missing piece, many pieces are discarded as too small or too large or not fitting, but, finally, It finds a piece which seems to fit well. After joining themselves, they experience the same circumstances in life that It had experienced previously. So It and the missing piece separate, and It . . . the story remains unfinished. One adolescent simply said, "Closed its mouth and found it was whole after all." Another has said, "And It was sad for the rest of its life." Another said, "It and the piece continued together, but not joined." Each of the answers gives an insight into the concerns, values, and commitments of the adolescents.

Committee-told Stories.—These are stories that unfold in the process of each participant adding the next incident. They permit teenagers to control events according to their own perspective. A story begins with the leader setting a context (a time, a place) and developing at least one character; then after a predetermined time, the story is picked up by a person to the right or the left. The story continues around the circle until everyone has had an opportunity to nurture the process for a few moments. Committee-told stories may or may not begin with the biblical setting, but they usually provide an opportunity to project adolescent situations for discussion.

One example of a committee-told story that usually brings a variety of interesting observations is about the dating and sexual values of a group. The story begins: Brett and Natasha met at a party through a mutual friend. After talking for a half hour, Brett suggested that they go for a ride. So they got in his car and . . . the next person picks up the story. After they've had an opportunity to fill in a segment of the vignette, the leader calls time, and the story continues with the next person. After all members have had an opportunity for whatever brief input they choose, the leader who began the story can bring the story to a conclusion, or the leader can simply drop the story with the last youth's input. It is important after a committee-told story to have ample time to process what happened in the story. Individuals can discuss their reaction to other persons' sense of direction and input into the story.

Take-your-pick Stories.—Take-your-pick stories call for direct value statements on the part of the teenagers. They are designed to facilitate discussion or to assess the value level of the adolescents. In Greek mythology, a hero is given an opportunity to choose wisdom, fame, or fortune. After telling the story, adolescents are given an opportunity to discuss which they would choose and why. Again, occasionally, I permit them to write their responses and then share with the group. Sometimes I have asked teenagers to divide into the wisdom group, the fame group, and the fortune group. As a group, they are to come up with the best possible defense for their choice. Then the groups have an opportunity to debate each other and discuss their responses. I found this an excellent exercise in working with parents and their own teenagers. The parents and teenagers have an opportunity to decide which they would choose and why.

Another form of the take-your-pick stories can be utilized with many of the biblical stories. An example is the story of Joseph and his brothers. After sharing it, ask teenagers to identify who they would choose to be like in the story. Surprisingly, a few teenagers regularly pick the slave trader as their hero in this story.

Contemporary versions of take-your-pick stories often center around situations where ethical decisions were unclear. For example, one group of teenagers responded positively to the story of a young engaged couple fleeing for their lives during World War II. As they were hiding in a barn, the enemy soldiers approached. For safety's sake, they hid in different places. She was found and became the object of adoring love with the enemy soldiers. They asked her if anyone else was in the barn. She could have lied to protect her fiancé, she could have responded to the affections of the soldier and given her fiancé time to escape, or she could have remained resistant and perhaps been killed. Teenagers were given an opportunity to ask what they would do if they were in the situation. They were also asked what they would want their fiancé to do if they were hiding and the one being protected. Although take-your-pick stories have their primary value for discussion in a small group of adolescents, they can be used in a one-on-one dialogue between an adult and a teenager. One is encouraged to think carefully through one's own response as an adult before using these types of stories with teenagers. Certainly, permitting teenagers to voice their views and listening to them will be important before sharing one's own views with the teenagers.

Role-play Stories.—Role-play stories use psychodrama to give adolescents an opportunity to participate in the making of a story or in the personalizing of a drama. For example, two adolescents might be asked to volunteer to be "father" and "mother" for a third adolescent when they would role-play the adolescent coming home late and trying to resolve the issue with the role-playing parents.

Three particularly helpful role plays have been used in a variety of contexts. First, I use a role play between two teenagers with one trying to introduce the other to substance abuse. I have had them trying to get another to try a beer or to smoke a joint or to experiment with hard drugs. The role plays permit the adolescents not only to sort through some of their values, but it gives them actual responses to use if the situation should come up later. A second productive role play involves the dating context. I have used role plays with everything from how to ask for a date to how to refuse a date to how to set limits on a physically aggressive dating partner to how to handle a potentially dangerous date. Many times, I will permit the teenagers doing the dating role play to call time-out and turn for coaching from their peers in the room. For example, the girl in the role play may call time-out and ask consultation from the other girls who are present. In a one-on-one context, I have played the other teenager in the role play in order to help a teenager work through some anxiety or to formulate actual thoughts as to how he or she would approach a given dating situation. A third productive role play involves teens admitting they have made a mistake to their parents or a teacher. Or a slight modification is a teenager being falsely accused by a parent or a teacher. Such a role play gives opportunity for adolescents to look at forgiving and the receiving of forgiveness, the handling of confidentialities, and the expression of the wide variety of feelings. A number of role plays can be developed and used with teenagers year after year. However, caution must be taken not to let the role plays become outdated.

Fun Stories

The fourth type, fun stories, are perhaps the most popular with teenagers. Teenagers enjoy poems, plays on words, and twisted definitions. They enjoy stories at fellowships that are entertaining and humorous. This is particularly true of older adolescents at the high school senior or college freshmen level. A variety of games and fun stories can be found in fellowship and retreat manuals, but a few of my favorites, which I believe are original, might be helpful for you.

Word Games.—I enjoy a game called "Making Up Old Chinese Proverbs." I begin the activities by telling a few stories from Oriental culture that end with a Chinese proverb. Then I suggest that we make up some Chinese proverbs. For example, "The father who does not play with his three-year-old will not have a thirteen-year-old around to play with." "The man who does not take his date seriously in college does not take her with him after college." "Grandchildren and grandparents get along so well together because they have a common enemy in the middle."

A second fun dialogue designed not only to entertain but to assist in understanding the values, commitments, and attitudes of a group of youth is what I call "Pun for the Money." This play on words challenges adolescents to make up a number of puns as a team and then share them with the entire group and have them rated one through ten by the group. A *one* deserves barely a chuckle; a *ten* has brought a belly laugh. We use a rather loose definition of *pun*, and many word plays are acceptable. One of my favorites is a triple pun: "Did you hear about the widow who named her ranch 'Focus' because it's where her sons raise meat?"

Some adolescents have grown up with Tom Swifties. We often switch from puns and give them an opportunity as individuals or teams to make up a "Tom Swifty" where the adverb carries double meaning. For example, "My pig has laryngitis," the farmer complained disgruntedly.

Still another is to challenge them to see how many definitions they can come up with for a given word. For example, "monologue—a single tree trunk or the illness journal of someone with mono." "Dialogue—how you get a purple log or the diary of someone on their deathbed." Such words games usually work best with well-educated teens such as a college group.

Humorous Stories.—I found many teens are attracted to speakers who can work puns or a turn in words into any of their presentations. They obviously are also attracted to humorous stories that relate to themselves. One of my favorites I first heard from Duke McCall, then president of The Southern Baptist Theological Seminary.

It seems that a young man was sent off to college by his father with traditional words of encouragement about doing well his first semester. He returned at Christmas break with a disgraceful grade card of three *F's* and a *D.* His father warned him if his grades did not improve to a *C* average the next semester that he would have to drop out of school and go to work in the family business.

Nothing frightens an eighteen-year-old like the words *go to work.* So the young man returned to campus filled with good intentions. He did what any bright eighteen-year-old would do. He asked his friends what were the easy courses. They told him that he would have to retake freshmen English since he had failed it, but it should be easier the second time around. One had noticed that the young man was fairly good at volleyball and suggested he might sign up for that in physical education. Another suggested that he sign up for chorus because he did have a pretty good voice. And one friend suggested that he take Ornithology 101. "Oh, he protested, "I've never been good at science. That sounds difficult." "No," assured the friend, "it's bird-watching, and old Prof Jones is so old and poor of sight that every class period is a field trip around campus. You describe the birds, and he rattles on about them. If you 'ooh' and 'aah' just a bit, you're assured of an *A.* You don't even have to show up every day because he's too blind to take class roll."

Armed with his new information, the young man entered the semester and was moving along quite well. He might not make a *C* in English, but he knew the ornithology would pull up his grade average. Sure enough, the old professor took them on field trips every day. Two weeks before the end of the semester, the prof had a stroke and was placed in the hospital. A young Ph.D. candidate was brought in to finish out the semester. The new professor was appalled at the ignorance of the students, declared there would be no more field trips, and that the entire final grade would rest on the final examination. He drilled the students with scientific information about birds—their beak structure, their feather types, their legs, feet, and body build. They learned the scientific names and classification of a multitude of birds.

The young man was devastated when he turned up to take the final exam and found that it was fifty pictures of birds from the knees down. They were to identify the bird and give as much information about it as they could. He was shocked. He recognized only one, and he wasn't sure if that was a duck or a goose. After a few frustrating moments, the student simply wadded up his paper, walked up to the young instructor, threw it on his desk, and said, "I don't have to take this," and turned to stomp out. The young professor called him back and said, "Young man, come here a minute. I don't have to take that from you either. What's your name?" To which the young man pulled up his pant leg to his knee, shook his foot at the young professor, and said, "You tell me," and walked out.

Such humorous stories can introduce a dialogue session in which one then turns to the adolescent and says, "This will be a you-tell-me session. I want to hear from you the kinds of problems that you are facing, or your reactions to this particular approach that's being taken in your church."

Fairy Tales.—Many other types of fun stories—ballads, songs, ghost stories, and fairy tales—can be used effectively with adolescents. A number of popular youth ministers retell fairy tales to give them a special meaning for adolescents. I have read perhaps four or five different versions of the frog and the princess and have added a few twists myself that I think are helpful to teenagers. When I retell the original fairy tale, it goes something like this:

A particularly mischievous prince was taunting and teasing the castle witch on a rainy day when it really wasn't feasible to test his skills in riding his favorite steed. The witch gave him ample warning by saying things like, "If you don't get out of here, you'll be sorry—I'll cast a spell on you. Now leave me alone." But the impulsive young prince could not resist irritating her even further. Finally, she zapped him and turned him into a frog, and she assured him that he would stay a frog until a beautiful princess kissed him. "That's no concern of mine," he croaked. "These chicks are always trying to make it with me."

He hopped over to the next castle, sure that the princess would kiss him. He explained the situation, promised to marry her and live happily ever after, only to find that she didn't believe him. In fact, he hopped from castle to castle throughout the kingdom, taking weeks, but he could find no one who would risk giving him a kiss.

Finally, the prince hopped back to his own castle, plopped down on a lily pad in the moat, and went to sleep. He was rudely awakened by a loud "kerplunk"! He turned over to see a giant, female frog eyeing him as only a princess had dared eye him before. He hopped to another lily pad; she followed! Finally, she said, "What's wrong with you?" "You see," he explained, "I'm not really a frog. I'm a prince in disguise." "Oh," she said, "what a coincidence! I'm a princess who was turned into a frog by a wicked sorcerer." *The story has gotten around,* he thought to himself. *Now she's using this on me. I can't believe her.*

So he debated and debated as she began to suggest that they might kiss. Finally, he convinced himself that if her story were true, maybe they could each transform the other. And if not, why it would cost him only one frog kiss. After all, that's what he had been asking others to do. He closed his eyes and puckered up, and as their lips met—presto! She became a beautiful princess, and he became the handsome prince that he had been before.

Now, teenagers, I know that I'm not relating the story according to the book. And I know that most of you, when you feel froggy, want a real prince or a real princess to kiss you. But my experience has been that taking a risk with someone who is aware of his or her frogginess is the first step toward mutual transformation. Few of us are going to find someone who has it all together stooping down to our level of selfhood. But if we will give ourselves to someone who has a lot in common with us, together we can participate in a personal identity transformation that will soon help others to see the prince and princess qualities that we see in each other.

This chapter has examined the art of storytelling by looking at how to, when, and why to tell stories. We have reviewed several types of stories—biblical stories, transformational stories, participation stories, and fun stories. Certainly you have your own repertoire of stories and your own approach to using stories with teenagers one-on-one or in groups. I encourage you to take this chapter as a springboard to share with some of your colleagues. And if you have a favorite story, send it to me. I'm still collecting.

3

Ethical Formation and Storytelling with Teens

Adolescent moral values reflect those of the adults in their lives. Some are admirable; some are not. Newspapers boldly broadcast teenagers' failures to live by the rules. Parents often complain that they can no longer trust their own teenagers. One mother said, "I know my daughter lies to me; I guess I've given up. I've stopped trying to catch her." Teachers remark that cheating on tests seems to be on the increase. Even youth reflect the lack of trust in their friends. A sixteen-year-old girl told me she was going to have a party, and she wasn't sending any invitations. She was only going to tell a few persons the day before the party. When I inquired as to why, she responded: "If word gets out, there's no telling who will come. And there's no way I can control them. My mother wouldn't begin to let me have a party if the kind of things went on that go on at most parties." Her lack of trust of her own peers reflects a sad awareness of the hedonistic tendencies of the large portion of adolescent culture.

Self-centeredness, indicative of a deep insecurity and lack of self-love, is in my opinion the primary cause of the lack of maturity in adolescent values. Insecure youth are grabbing at straws for a sense of identity as they drown in the confusion of who they really are. Their values come more from movies, TV shows, and music than from traditional sources such as home, school, and church. A large portion of the youth culture operates at a low level, according to Lawrence Kohlberg's stages of moral development.

The story of Cain and Abel aptly illustrates the kind of teenage self-centeredness that leads to moral disruption. Cain killed his brother Abel when God found Abel's offering more favorable. Cain could not tolerate being less than the center of God's devotion. Jealousy betrays a lack of self-confidence and a deep-seated loss of the center of selfhood. Adolescents who feel, like Cain, that they are unacceptable and not the center of their world often turn to behaviors that draw criticism. The criticism comes not only from adult authority figures but also from their peers. Teenagers who turn to self-indulgence show a disrespect for the feelings, property, and rights of others. While they are attempting to find a sense of security, they are bringing on themselves condemnation and judgment from parents, teachers, and peers and from themselves when they reflect on their own lack of self-worth.

Humans are not born with a set of moral values, but they are born into a context of moral values. As children grow, they seldom rise above the moral value of their family. One youth arrested numerous times by the time he was sixteen confessed to his chaplain that he realized he was born into a family of thieves and that he wanted to break free. After a religious conversion experience, he found a new community in the family of God at his church and was able to modify his own moral thinking and subsequent behavior. He rose above the moral values of his family. Without outside assistance, few youth will rise above the moral values of their family.

I recall vividly my surprise at the open disregard for authority and the personal embracing of a "if-it-benefits-me, why-not-do-it?" philosophy of life. Soon after my twin sons turned thirteen, I was chauffeuring them and three of their schoolmates to a musical program at the Center for the Arts downtown. They were to receive extra credit in one of their courses at school for having attended and were to validate their attendance by bringing a program for the activity. As we were leaving the theater, one of the other youth reached over and picked up a stack of programs. Naively I asked, "Did you really like it so much that you want to keep some souvenirs?"

"No," she boldly replied. "I'll get a dollar apiece for these before school tomorrow."

"You're not going to sell them! That wouldn't be fair," came my response.

"Fair!" she said, "Why, it will help my friends get better grades, and I'll make some dough, too. It seems like a good idea to me. I'm sure I won't get caught—unless, of course, you're going to rat on me," she protested.

Her moral decision making was based on what was good for her and what she projected would be good for her friends. She thought it would be good for her friends to receive better grades. Little did she realize that they were ultimately being cheated.

Studying fifty adults over a period of nearly twenty years, Lawrence Kohlberg developed a six-phase description of the moral development of humans. These stages have been observed in several other cultures and stand the test as universal development of moral decision-making process. The stages focus on the motivation and process of decision making, not so much on the behavior and the decision that a person makes. It's possible to do the right thing but for the wrong reasons. How one makes decisions about what's right and wrong ultimately reflects the level of moral development.

Stages of Moral Development in Adolescents

Delinquent adolescents operate at a level of moral decision making different from that of adolescents who have not been institutionalized or sent before the court system. The delinquent adolescents operate on what Kohlberg has called the preconventional level while nondelinquent adolescents are capable of operating at the conventional level. Few if any teenagers would ever be expected to reach the postconventional level of moral development. This is a level of development usually attained only in adult life. Each of the three levels of moral development—preconventional, conventional, and postconventional—have two stages, thus producing six possible stages. As people mature, Kohlberg has observed that they move through the stages at varied speeds according to their education, their awareness of themselves, their sensitivity to other persons, and what we would generally consider to be religious education. It is possible to have characteristics of two of the stages. Persons might be moving from stage one into stage two and show some of the characteristics of each. However, people have not demonstrated characteristics of stages at three different levels. When indications of two levels have been found, it has been two adjacent levels (for example, two and three or three and four), never two nonadjacent levels (for example, one and three or two and four).

Kohlberg also found that moral reasoning never occurred at advanced stages before persons had developed at the more fundamental stages. All adults who reach the postconventional stages had gone through preconventional and conventional.

In order to move from stage to stage, people have to be unsettled and motivated to reflect on their current decision-making process. Larry Henderson, who researched delinquent adolescents' responses to stories for moral stage development, said youth must be challenged to think about the process and see where there are weaknesses in their thinking in order to make decisions through a different process. He proposed stories as an effective way of causing them to rethink their process of decision making. In fact, a group of teens who participated in an ongoing religious education story group for three months significantly increased their level of moral awareness and reflected a much lower rate of getting in trouble later on (Henderson, 71). Teenagers who experience a reversal or a sense of unfairness through a story can be led to rethink their own moral values and decision-making process.

In stages one and two, a sense of something not being fair or being according to the rules brings about a level of cognitive uneasiness. Usually this level of thinking is reserved for children, but some adolescents fail to escape the doing-whatever-one-can-get-away-with kind of mentality. Obeying the parents' authority in childhood changes to testing the limits in adolescence. A personal moral code is developed and lived out in adulthood. The patterns of adolescent moral development originate in childhood and may carry through to adulthood unless through stories they are modified as the teenagers' level of development matures. Modification can happen basically through two types of stories. If stories are told in a way that adolescents can identify with them and discuss them, then the teens may change their process of moral reasoning. The story can be the youth's own life history if a parent, youth minister, or counselor can assist the adolescent to reflect on problems. They can examine moral alternatives, rethink the context, and decide to act differently in the future.

For example, a teenager arrested for stealing a car realized his so-called friends had used him; they set him up to go along with them and then let him drive the car. When they were pulled over by the police, the friends all ran, and he was left with the car and took the rap. None of his "friends" came forward to stand up with him. In rethinking this incident he was able to see that his friends' level of morality had been, "We won't get caught, nothing bad's going to happen to us." He realized after discussing the issue at some length that physical harm could have come to him or his friends. Several months later he could even say that taking the car was harming the owner and her family.

The moral stages as given below need to be discussed at some length with adolescents.

Kohlberg's Levels of Moral Development

Level	Stage	Ethical Patterns
Preconventional	1	Ethical decisions are made by doing what persons in power dictate in order to avoid punishment. As long as you don't "get caught," it's OK.
Preconventional	2	Moral decisions center on being responsible for oneself, and one's own needs; this leaves others to be responsible for themselves. This is a you-scratch-my-back, I'll-scratch-your-back kind of decision making.
Conventional	3	Moral decisions are based on a higher level of good. Doing what is right for others as well as what is right for self means living by a common moral code. Teenagers might reflect this in statements like, "Well put yourself in my shoes," or, "Look at it from their point of view."

Conventional	4	Moral decisions seek to maintain the values of society. The welfare of the group is taken into account. Teenagers might say something like, "If everybody did it, it wouldn't be good for our country," or, "I can make this sacrifice because I know it's best for the entire church."
Postconventional	5	Moral decisions emphasize individual rights and freedom within a society; the only limits are society's general rules. Moral right is seen as a social contract. Adults would be expected to live by this code and might reflect it with a statement like, "I live in a way that upholds the Constitution of the United States."
Postconventional	6	Moral decisions are based on an obligation to higher principles applying to all people, even to those outside our society. Principles of respect for all persons are based on justice, equality, and love. Adults at this stage might reflect a need to work to change their social contract in order to bring justice to persons even outside their own social groups.

Examples of Moral Development

As we discuss the first four stages of development in relationship to adolescents, we can easily see typical behavior in each of these stages.

Preconventional: Stage One

Adolescents in the obedience-authority or don't-get-caught stage of morality frequently congregate in street gangs or other violent behavior groups. While they might ascribe to some level of internal morality in their gang, usually that behavior is controlled only by the intimidation of the gang leader. Nevertheless, an individual adolescent who perpetrates crimes alone could also be at this basic level of morality.

The Old Testament story of Cain and Abel demonstrates how Cain's jealous rage caused him to rebel against moral authority. Cain's primary concern was not remorse but hiding his sin from God. Not getting caught seemed more important than doing what was right. The result of Cain's moral disobedience was being branded and cast as a vagrant and a wanderer on the face of the earth (Gen. 4:12).

Preconventional: Stage Two

Adolescents in the second stage of preconventional morality might be seen as participating in less violent but still antisocial behavior. They could well be assisting each other in cheating on examinations, participating in the buying and selling of stolen goods, or telling lies to mutually cover inappropriate behavior before each other's parents. This you-do-something-for-me-and-I'll-do-something-for-you sense of fairness reflects an egocentric preoccupation with self and a lack of concern particularly for those outside of the group.

While we certainly would not condone the action of Joseph's brothers when they sold him into slavery rather than kill him, that was a step above Cain. Their giving of Joseph as a slave in return for payment was a you-do-something-for-me, we'll-do-something-for-you relationship with the slave traders.

Conventional: Stage Three

Adolescents in the third stage of moral development can see the overall sense of having good motives. Also, they are able to avoid most antisocial behavior by putting themselves in the victim's shoes and realizing they would not want to be treated that way. Such behavior is typical of younger adolescents, and they are the backbone of our church groups, school clubs, and organizations that are committed to doing what is right. Certainly the clearest expression of this level of morality is expressed in the Golden Rule: "Do unto others as you would have them do unto you."

Conventional: Stage Four

The fourth level of moral development can be seen in a few mature adolescents who are committed to maintaining the rules of a group or society in order to benefit the larger group. These individuals can sacrificially set aside their own well-being, personal desires, and needs for the benefit of the group. Such adolescents are the leaders of a youth group or school club. They are the ones who are willing to sacrificially give of their time in order to better the other youth in the church or school. They would be the persons who would do what is right as a witness to other youth. Joseph, as a young man, may have withstood the seductive temptations of Potiphar's wife through this level of morality (Gen. 39). He was willing to suffer imprisonment rather than to violate the rules of morality. Later he more clearly demonstrated this view of morality when he explained to his brothers that their intent to harm him had been used by God for good because he was now able to give them food in a time of famine.

Adolescents would not be expected to reach stages five or six of moral development; however, we see these stages in several biblical accounts. Moral rightness is based in stage five on the individual rights of a person in a society and can be seen clearly in the Sermon on the Mount where a sense of justice is maintained with high ideals. Stage six where moral rightness is commitment to principles applying to all humankind was clearly summarized by Jesus in His statement of the greatest commandments: "Thou shalt love the Lord thy God with all thy heart, and with all thy soul, and with all thy mind," and "Thou shalt love thy neighbor as thyself" (Matt. 22:37,39, KJV). Such an ethic calls for all persons to live by principles of social justice and equality regardless of concern for self or one's own group.

Let us now examine some stories and the way they can be used in facilitating our communication with adolescents. The twofold purpose of these stories is to assist in assessing the development stage of the youth and to facilitate the person's movement toward the next higher stage. These suggestions can be used in individual dialogue between parents and their own youth or in study groups with teachers and a number of adolescents. While it is best to have a like-minded group for the sake of discussion, having an age, social, economic, and educational diversity seems to produce enough tension and dissonance that members are more willing to change their moral values over a period of time.

Ethical Stories

Story One

A story used widely by Kohlberg in *The Just Community Approach to Corrections* might be helpful in knowing which stage an adolescent might be reflecting. A leader would tell the following story and then ask students to take a sheet of paper and answer seven questions. They can either share their written answers with the leader privately or they can share their answers one question at a time with group discussion. Some youth may reflect a transition between the stages and have elements of each. The stages would be adjacent. They do not skip a stage.

Joe is a fourteen-year-old boy who wanted to go to camp very much. His father promised him he could go if he saved up his money. So Joe worked at his paper route and saved the $40 it cost to go to camp, and a little more besides. But just before the camp was to start, Joe's father changed his mind. Some of his friends decided to go on a special fishing trip, and Joe's father was short of the money it would cost. So he told Joe to give him the money he had saved from the paper route. Joe didn't want to give up the money for camp, so he thought of refusing to give his father the money.

Questions.—Should Joe refuse to give his father the money? Why or why not?

Is there any way in which the father has a right to tell his son to give up his money? Why or why not?

What is the most important thing a father should recognize in his relationship to his son? What makes you say that?

What is the most important thing a son should recognize in his relationship to his father? What makes you say that?

Should promises always be kept? Why or why not?

What makes a person feel bad when a promise is broken?

Is it important to keep a promise to someone you don't know well or someone you're not very close to? Why or why not?

Story Two

Another story that gives adolescents an opportunity to discuss their responses to a situation was used by Chaplain Larry Henderson in the treatment program of the Arkansas Boys' Home (Henderson, 65).

A wealthy farmer was out hunting one night with his favorite coon dogs. After a successful hunt, he collected all of his dogs except two. He searched for over an hour, but he finally gave up and returned to the house with his other dogs. The next day he asked around for help in locating his dogs. His teenage son voluntarily searched the woods all day and way into the night. After nearly twenty-four hours, the boy found one of the dogs. He was exhausted, scratched, hungry, and bruised from his search. Soon after the boy returned with the dog, another man arrived with the other dog in the back of his pickup truck. The second man explained that the coon dog had wandered into his yard and was searching for food. The owner was extremely happy to have both of his hounds returned. He gave the man in the pickup truck and the boy who had searched all day $20 each. The man in the truck thanked the owner and departed. The son became angry, went to his room, and pouted. He thought he should have received a larger reward because he had worked harder to find the dog.

Questions.—Should the son have received more money than the neighbor? Why or why not?

Did the boy have a right to get angry? Why or why not?

Should the farmer do anything about the boy's feelings? If so, why?

What would you have done if you were the boy? Why?

Story Three

Matthew 18:24-35 provides an excellent discussion story for adolescents. A paraphrase of the story might be as follows:

A king who wished to settle an account with his servants began the process of checking their books. He brought a servant before him who owed ten thousand dollars. The servant said he could not pay the account. The king ordered him to be sold along with his wife and children and all that he had so that some payment could be made. The servant fell to his knees and begged: "Lord, have patience with me. I will pay you everything eventually." Out of pity for him, the king released the servant and forgave him the debt. He owed nothing.

That very same servant went to one of his fellow servants who owed him one hundred dollars. He seized the fellow servant by the throat and said, "Pay me what you owe." This fellow servant fell to his knees and began to beg. "Have patience with me, and I will repay you." The first servant refused, and had the other man thrown into prison until his family could pay the debt.

When the other servants saw what had taken place, they were upset and reported this to the king. The king summoned the first servant again and said, "You wicked man! I forgave you your debt because you pleaded with me. Why didn't you forgive your fellow servant's debt?" In anger, the king sent him to jail until his family could repay his debt.

Questions.—Did the first servant have the right to collect his money since the king had forgiven his debts? Why or why not?

What would you have done if you had been the king? Why?

Was it right for the other servants to report the first servant to the king? Why or why not?

What would you have done if you had been the first servant?

What would you have done if you had been the second servant?

Story Four

The following contemporary story provides several points of departure for discussion with youth. Not only will they have an opportunity to examine their ethical foundation, but they will also have the opportunity to consider the possibility that what they think is right or wrong will not necessarily keep them from doing wrong. A lack of self-control and the inability to understand one's feelings may cause one to live at a level below one's moral convictions.

Janice was fidgeting with her long, flowing blonde hair as she mumbled, "I really don't know why I came to talk with you." Her words cracked and faded into quiet sobbing. I waited as she began again. "You see, I've done something so awful. I've hurt my boyfriend so very much. Uh, uh, uh . . . I don't know why I did it. I can't believe I did it. It's so stupid, it's not me," she cried out. "How could I have done something like that?" she almost pleaded with herself. "I feel so dirty and guilty," she continued.

"Back up a few steps," I replied. "Tell me what this is all about." Although Janice had not specifically told me what she had done, I could begin to imagine what she meant. Still, I wanted to hear her story and thereby perhaps aid her in discovering some answers to her own questions. If she could discover her own answers, she would have a better understanding of herself.

Janice wiped her nose, and her big blue eyes sparkled through the tears as she began to explain how she and Jim had started dating the past summer. "Jim's family is rather wealthy, and his father is a powerful man in this community," she partially boasted. "His parents treated me like a daughter, until all of this," she muttered. "Now his mom won't even speak with me. His dad told me to get out of Jim's life and leave them alone. I've just ruined everything," Janice confessed.

"What do you mean, 'all of this' has 'ruined everything'?" I inquired.

"Well," she paused, "it all started, I guess, when I told Jim that I didn't want to go to a movie on Friday night because my neighbors were having a going-away party, and they wanted me to be there. These were kids I had grown up with. Jim said he didn't want to go because he wouldn't know any of the people, and he would be bored. He really doesn't respect my neighborhood very much. He had been getting rather bossy and domineering and even pushy lately; I didn't like that, so this time I decided I wasn't going to give in. I insisted I was going and told him he could go if he wanted to," she continued. "Well, he came, but he acted like a stuffed toad. He hardly spoke to anyone, and he was rude when I introduced him to my friends. As soon as the gifts were opened, he wanted to skip the refreshments and leave. I said no. I suppose that embarrassed him or something, so he got mad and walked out. He said, 'Some of your friends can take you home.' I thought he would come back, but he didn't," Janice added sadly.

"And that's it? He got upset just because you wanted to stay at the party?"

"No," she said. "After about an hour, this new boy, the brother of one of my friends, started talking to me. He asked me what happened to Jim, and I told him he got upset and left. The new guy, Brook, said he would take me home. I don't know why I even agreed; I wouldn't normally let a stranger take me home. But I did."

"Oh, Jim got upset because of Brook?" I asked.

After a painful pause, Janice said, "That's not all. You see Brook did not take me straight home. He suggested we could go over to his older brother's apartment and listen to this new CD he had bought on the way to the party. I knew I should have said no. But for some strange reason I didn't. Oh, how I wish I had said no," Janice said half aloud and half to herself. "Well, he gave me a couple of drinks; I know I shouldn't have tried them, but I wanted to act big, so I drank them. Then he started kissing me, and we started making out, and, well, you know, we went too far." Janice looked up with a strange expression and added, "I was so upset when he took me home. I told my parents everything that happened. I don't know why I did that. They were furious and told me I was grounded for a month and that I could never see Brook again. Of course, that was fine with me; I never wanted to see him in the first place."

"Did your parents tell Jim? Surely they wouldn't have."

"No," Janice replied, "when I told Jim I had been grounded for a month, he knew something big had happened. For a week I told him it was just that I let Brook bring me home, and we were late. But he continued to quiz me, and I broke down and told him everything. Jim went to pieces. He was so hurt and so broken up. He was devastated. He talked with his dad; his mom knows; and now everybody thinks I'm awful. I guess they're right. Why did I let this whole mess happen?" she pleaded.

Questions.—OK, you answer Janice's questions.

How did she get into such a mess?

Why is she so down on herself?

A month earlier she was a fun-loving, highly respected leader in her church youth group. Why did she trade that for all this mess?

Possible Answers.—Some of you might respond to these questions: "Alcohol! When she took those drinks she lost control of her ability to judge for herself." Perhaps that's correct. Remember, however, she did say she knew better than to go to the apartment in the first place. At least some of her judgment was restricted at that point. Her ability to do what she knew was right was lost before the first taste of alcohol. It probably worsened it, but it wasn't the only cause.

Others of you might say, "It was the wrong crowd. She got with the wrong kind of boy, and he got her into this mess." Sure, that's probably a part of what happened to Janice. But she didn't go to the party with the wrong crowd. She went to the party with her trusted boyfriend Jim. She didn't even know Brook before the party. She didn't choose him; he just offered to take her home. She normally would not have gone home with a stranger, but she broke that rule. Why? "Oh," you might say, "it was her boyfriend's fault for leaving her stranded in the first place. He set her up to get into trouble." OK. Jim did treat her badly. He acted like a spoiled brat, but he certainly didn't intend for her to get into such a mess. In fact, he was devastated by what happened.

Consider another possibility. Consider that Janice lost control of herself because of her pent-up anger. She was so mad that she stopped thinking clearly and started acting impulsively. She was angry for many reasons. First, Jim did not want to go with her to the party. Second, he was acting rudely. Third, he left her stranded. Fourth, she had been angry for a little while because he had been too bossy and pushy toward her. She chose not to confront Jim with her anger but tried to hide it. Her repressed feelings, like a balloon, got bigger and bigger after she swallowed them. Her anger got so strong that she stopped thinking clearly and started acting without any self-control. Janice let her anger take charge of her. She didn't know it at the time, but later she would see that she was trying to hurt Jim and maybe get even by paying some attention to Brook. Of course, Janice didn't choose to get into trouble, but she let her anger put her in a position where she could get into trouble. Sometimes even when we know right from wrong, if we lose control we still might not do the right thing. Janice paid a very high price to learn that lesson. Her self-discovery of her anger soon led to some new understanding, and in counseling Janice was able to expand her capacity to do what she knew was right.

Questions for Reflection.—Did Janice have a right to be angry with Jim? Why or why not? If you were Jim, what would you have done when Janice wouldn't leave the party? If you were Janice, would you have gone home with Brook? Why or why not? What other choices did she have? If you were Janice, would you have gone to the apartment? Why or why not? Would you have taken a drink? Why or why not? Would you have told your parents? Why or why not?

What should happen to Brook? Why? Were Janice's parents right in grounding her? Should Janice have told Jim? Why or why not? Should Jim have told his parents? Why or why not? Did his parents have a right to treat Janice in this way? Why or why not?

As teens discuss stories, they can test their own ethical formation and perhaps grow in their capacity to make clear moral decisions through identifying with the characters in a number of different stories. Parents, you will undoubtedly have stories from your own teenage years—stories when you perhaps struggled with difficult decisions. Consider sharing them with your youth and discuss their reactions. Be careful that you don't preach at them. Listen, talk, and learn together.

If you work regularly with adolescents, different crises will come up in the youth group. When teens are talking about such an experience, take time to reflect on it and use the story as an opportunity for teaching and understanding moral behavior. Be careful not to violate any confidentiality and maintain a good open dialogue with the youth.

A deeper level of using stories with adolescents involves conversations privately or in small groups designed to assist the young person toward self-understanding and self-awareness. Weekly conversations with Janice in the previous story assisted her in discovering her anger and in learning not to be so controlled by it. These deeper conversations utilized storytelling in a more personal, direct way. Let us turn our attention to the living stories of the adolescents in our world and consider ways of becoming involved in assisting these teenagers to rewrite those stories in light of the gospel story.

4

Living Stories and Counseling with Teenagers

A valued colleague, respected nationally for his scholarship, stopped by my office for casual conversation. I soon became aware that something else was on his mind. He began to unfold a frequently reported story about his teenage son. The son, fifteen years old, had experienced a devastating rejection from a girlfriend. The father had noticed over a period of several days that the boy was not himself. The youth would come in from school and go straight to his room. He appeared at the table to eat, but he said little and then quickly returned to his room. When his best friend showed up and suggested they play some soccer, for the first time in the father's memory the son refused to go play; instead he went back to his room. The father, naturally concerned for his son, decided they needed to have a talk. After getting through several awkward moments and hearing "I don't know" and "I'm not sure why," the father finally convinced the son that he cared enough to know what was going on.

As the son told how he had been rejected by the special girl, the father found an appropriate time to share some of his own early hurt as a teenager just beginning to date. Their conversation seemed to leave the son feeling somewhat better, but the father said, "I'm still troubled." I inquired about the nature of his troubled feelings. "You see," he said, "I know it's normal to feel down and depressed when a boy loses his girlfriend. But how do I know if this is a serious depression? How can I tell if he's in trouble or if this is something he will snap out of in a short time?" The father's questions were not unusual.

"I'm really concerned for my daughter Christy," confessed a new member of our church. She went on to tell how Christy's behavior had changed radically during the last six months. Christy had begun staying out past her curfew, grossly abusing her phone privileges, and her grades had tumbled. She had begun dating a young man who had not finished high school and was five years older than she. Christy was becoming sarcastic and disrespectful with her mother and started spending more and more time alone in her room. "Is she just going through a phase? Will the rebellion stop if I ignore it?" the mother inquired. Of course, I needed to talk with the mother and Christy before I could begin to answer these questions, but I assured her that once I heard Christy's story then we could decide in which direction we would need to move. Christy turned out to be very concerned about her parents' filing for divorce. She regained control of her life as the family talked openly about her concerns.

Parents are not the only persons attempting to assess the level of trouble of teenagers. Youth ministers, Sunday School teachers, pastors, pastors' spouses—anyone who works with youth—can have a question about the well-being of a particular teenager. "I am concerned for Nicki," a minister's wife recently confided. Nicki had been quarreling with her parents for several weeks, and she had refused to get her hair trimmed when her mother informed Nicki she had made an appointment for her. The mother gave Nicki the car keys and told her she must go to get her hair trimmed. As she walked out the door, in anger Nicki yelled over her shoulder, "I might just get it shaved!" "Go ahead and see if I care," the mother retorted sarcastically. When Nicki returned, the mother was appalled to find that she had indeed gotten half of her hair shaved and the other half barely trimmed.

Nicki was shunned by some of her friends at school and church. Other kids who had never talked with her identified with her statement of rebellion and came up to tell her how proud they were that she could make her statement. Nicki was confused, hurt, and ashamed. She wasn't sure why she had impulsively gotten her hair cut as she did, but she was sure that she didn't like many of the reactions from her peers and from some adults. The minister's wife questioned, "How can we tell if Nicki is in serious difficulty and needs help?"

Story Dimensions

Parents, teachers, and ministers who are watching the living stories of teenagers in their world can explore a few basic dimensions of the teenager's situation and have some general feeling as to how serious the situation might be. In order to recall these aspects of the situation, we will look at them in alphabetical order.

Age Appropriateness

The first is *age appropriateness*. One must ask if a given behavior can be expected of an adolescent of this particular age. Anxiety about dating and the fear of talking to members of the opposite sex, for example, would be more appropriate for a thirteen- or fourteen-year-old than for an eighteen- or nineteen-year-old. Worry and concern about what vocation one is going to choose and what one will do for a living, on the other hand, is more appropriate to an eighteen- or nineteen-year-old than it would be to a thirteen- or fourteen-year-old. The young man discussed earlier who was depressed over the rejection from his girlfriend would be exhibiting age-appropriate behavior. This was his first rejection and breakup with a girlfriend. He would be expected to take this harder and would not be expected to know how to deal with such situations with ease. Therefore, we might judge his situation as not dangerous or serious.

Brutalizing Perspective

How *brutalizing* was the experience or is the problem from the adolescent's perspective? The intensity of the problem from the youth's viewpoint helps us evaluate its seriousness. A problem that bruises the very sense of self and strips the adolescent of confidence, respect, or personal security can be devastating. However, if the problem is not too bad and the adolescent realizes that it's more of a scratch on the surface of his or her security, then one would not respond with alarm. Nicki should be taken quite seriously because when she shaved half of her head, her own sense of self was shattered. She didn't realize the intensity of the reaction from others, that some people would reject her, or that she would feel so devastated and embarrassed in public.

Change from the Norm

Change is a third aspect of a situation to be examined. Ask yourself how big of a departure from the norm a given situation would be. If it is a radical change of behavior for an adolescent, this could indicate that more serious and pervasive problems exist. Students who have been making *A's* and *B's* and come home one semester with failing grades indicate that something fairly serious has happened. However, if a student's grades drift from *A* to *C* over a period of two or three years, this might not indicate an intense immediate problem. Christy's rebellion against her mother was not a radical change from her previous behavior. She had never been an overly compliant child, and as a teenager she had become somewhat testy over a period of time. Although her sassy, sarcastic comebacks were certainly unacceptable, they did not represent a radical change from her previous personality.

Duration of the Problem

Duration of the problem is another factor that helps determine the severity of the issue. If a problem has continued without getting any better for a significant period of time, then the parents, teachers, or youth ministers would want to suggest professional help. In the case of the depressed teenage boy, his depression had only been going on about a week and had already started getting somewhat better. Since this was of a relatively brief duration, professional help would not be indicated. If, however, the depression continued for a month and he still was unable to perform in school, was unwilling to relate to his family, and was isolating himself in his room, then counseling with a trained individual would be a good idea.

Extensiveness of the Problem

Extensiveness refers to how much of the person's life is affected by the circumstance. One might ask how many areas of life are being impacted by the situation. Was it affecting relationship to family, relationship to peers, or relationship to church? How did it affect school, extracurricular activities, and hobbies? Examining the pervasiveness of the problem provides insight into its severity. Nicki was being affected in all areas of her life by her impulsive decision to shave half of her head. Her family seemed to understand, but they still saw the haircut as a symbol of her anger. Some of her closest friends at school did not understand at all and actually began to reject her. Other school friends and new people she met began to treat her as if she were weird. Her grades were suffering. Her boyfriend did not understand, and it seemed as if this were the only thing she could talk about. Fortunately for her, she did have a teacher who was willing to stay by her during her predicament. If her situation showed other signs of crisis beyond the extensiveness, she might need soon to talk with a counselor.

Faith Realism

A youth's *faith* stance provides a further clue to the severity of any emergency that might present itself. Realistic faith does not assume that everything will care for itself, nor does it write off God as having little or nothing to offer in the crisis. When hearing a youth's story of personal plight, try to understand how faith relates to life from their perspective. Do they see God as a realistic source of strength, a God who will suffer with and sustain them? Or do they see God as detached and unconcerned? Do they view themselves as having a role to play in the outcome of the circumstance, or do they avoid all personal responsibility under the pretense of trusting God?

Christy said she wasn't sure how God related to her parents' divorce and her feelings about it. She supposed God didn't really care. While a part of her stance may reflect an anger at God, further inquiry revealed she really did not know God as friend and personal sustainer. Her knowledge of God far exceeded her experiences with God.

Groundedness in Reality

Another indicator of the severity of a teenager's well-being is how *grounded* in reality the teenager seems to be. Often youth will distort the severity of a problem in either direction. Some may underestimate its severity. This is particularly true with chemical dependency, while others overreact to the severity of the problem, as might be the case with the loss of a boyfriend or a girlfriend. Assessing the groundedness of a teenager's point of view about his or her situation can be difficult unless one has access to data from other sources. Talking with parents, listening to the teen's peers, and rechecking with the teenager are all means of assessing the groundedness of the teenager's interpretations of a given crisis. Christy maintained herself with the fantasy that she would be able to manipulate her parents to get back together. She was unwilling to accept the reality of their impending divorce. While her crisis was fairly intense as it was, her interpretation was not grounded in reality, indicating that her crisis could worsen if she did not receive help in adjusting to her parents' divorce.

Hope for the Future

Hope, an additional factor to survey, refers to the adolescent's stance toward the future. A number of adolescents do not expect their context to improve. They do not think in terms of alternatives, they sincerely believe that things will get no better. Not infrequently, adolescents will make statements like "I'm never going to get out of this," "Nothing can help," and, "This is impossible." The degree of hope as over against hopelessness is an effective measure of the severity of an adolescent's crisis. As long as there is hope, the teenager will continue to struggle toward wholeness. While Nicki had little immediate hope that the response of her family and friends to her radical head shaving would improve, she did express a long-term hope by saying half humorously, "At least it will grow out. Someday I'll be able to look back on this and laugh." Humor oftentimes reflects a hopeful stance as an adolescent faces difficult predicaments. Nicki's teacher was helping her come up with some humorous replies when shocked individuals asked, "What happened to your hair?" They decided she could say things like "I had a half a mind to get a haircut," "I saw a sign that said haircuts half price," or, "I'm modeling for a shampoo commercial, it won't take too long."

Isolation Appraisal

Isolation is an additional factor to be appraised in determining the severity of an adolescent's crisis. The strength of a teen's social network can be more significant than the strength of the family network. This is especially true for older adolescents. One way of getting at the degree of isolation is to ask, "Who are your best friends? How often do you see them? What kinds of things do you share?" Frequently, a troubled adolescent will either be unable to name a best friend or identify someone who lives out of town or a person they have not seen for a number of months. The lack of peer support signals that the youth's crisis is more intense. Finding ways to help the youth make friends can be a significant ministry. Be cautious that in assessing a youth's degree of isolation you do not misjudge participation for attachment. It is possible for a youth to attend a group meeting like a Sunday School class and still be very isolated. They can feel lonely even in the crowd. Christy particularly felt isolated. Her best friend had moved over five hundred miles away, she had attended a new school nearly a semester, and she had no one she could call a good friend. She fantasized marriage with a young man, although she had had only a few dates with him. Her pathetic sense of aloneness signaled the need for immediate assistance. While family support may not always be as significant as peer support for older adolescents, in assessing isolation one still needs to examine the bonds between the teenager, his or her parents or stepparents, and siblings. Often examining the relationship to grandparents can also yield fruitful information. While the depressed young man's rejection by his girlfriend was certainly painful, the fact that he could eventually talk with his father is a positive sign. Feeling the love and support of a kinship group facilitates growth with youth. When youth are in a crisis, one good indicator of the possibility that they will completely recover is the level of concern and support from their immediate family.

Hopefully, these *ABC's* of assessing the severity of teenagers' problems can serve as a guideline as you listen to their stories and try to decide whether they simply need someone with whom they can share or need professional help (or both). As you make the determination, your judgment will be tested, and perhaps it is best that you consult with one or two adults that you know, respect, and trust. It is difficult to determine precisely when a teenager has crossed the line from typical growing pains to a crisis that needs special attention.

Telling Your Story and Mine

As youth recount their stories, we undoubtedly identify at many points. As we listen, we need to maintain caution and not overidentify with them and miss the uniqueness of their stories. As teenagers share a series of events, listen carefully for how they are making sense out of life. Ask yourself what are their unspoken assumptions about the way life works or doesn't work for them. Inasmuch as possible, bracket your own life experience and hear the context of each teenager's story in its uniqueness. Just as each individual is created in an original pattern, all life stories are dissimilar from one other.

Since adolescence represents such a significant transition for all of us, we face a powerful temptation to tell similar stories from our past before teenagers are finished with their stories. Patient listening and careful exploration of detail soon lead us to understand the disparity between their stories and our stories. No two adolescent experiences are identical. Hearing the new, novel side of their stories convinces them that we value them as important. Hastily jumping in with comments like "I know how that feels," or "I remember when that happened to me" cuts off the dialogue and discounts their situation.

While there are certainly a number of nearly universal adolescent experiences (male/female attraction, relationships to parents, and developing a sense of self-identity), one must exert effort to maintain the originality and individuality of each story. After hearing out the teenager's situation, one may wish to request permission to share a brief personal vignette. My professional colleague effectively shared with his son and found the son's awareness that his father had broken relationships prior to meeting and marrying his mother was helpful.

Frequently, an adult will hear a teenager's story and realize that the youth belongs to a clique or subgroup unlike or even opposite to that in which the adult participated as a youth. Nicki's teacher realized that Nicki belonged to a radical subgroup that regularly questioned authority and openly rejected the preppy kids in her school. Although the teacher herself had been somewhat preppy as an adolescent, she was able to set that aside and understand Nicki's anger toward such students in her school. After sharing briefly about one's own adolescence, perhaps an adolescent story from the Scripture can effectively communicate with most teenagers. As discussed in chapter 2, a variety of biblical stories can be utilized to assist teenagers in identifying with the universal nature of their struggle. However, sharing biblical stories and the gospel story, in particular, can have a prescriptive function with youth. They can see the moral teaching and sense an element of hope that otherwise would not be present.

If teenagers are somewhat familiar with the Bible, I have found it effective to ask for their favorite Bible stories or favorite Bible characters. We actually read the story together, and then I ask them to relate it in whatever ways possible to their current situation. To our amazement, new insights begin to surface, and the Bible story serves to integrate our stories into new patterns of meaning. The integrative function of biblical stories strengthens adolescents' understanding of themselves as well as their appreciation for the Scripture.

Let us consider a few living stories that can assist teenagers in understanding their own situations.

A Story of Hope

White fluffy clouds dotted the otherwise clear blue autumn sky. *Such afternoons are perfect for harvesting,* David reflected silently as he began collecting the golden grain from his own private, ten-acre plot on the family farm. His heart pounding, he rammed the corn picker into the first rows and watched the glittering kernels begin to spill into the trailing wagon. Fantasies of how he would spend his profits were suddenly shaken by a thud. He knew the picker was blocked. *Perhaps I hit a limb from that old oak tree that stands guard over the fence row,* he thought to himself. *Maybe I was moving too fast through the rows, or worst of all,* he concluded, *the machinery could be broken.* David stopped and climbed down from his commanding perch above the rows of grain and turned to pull the clogged stalks from the machine. He did not see his father coming across the field to help. Suddenly a nightmare began.

The stalks broke loose, and the machine started up. His shirt sleeve was caught in the picker, and before he could respond, his hand, wrist, and arm were pulled into the thrashing jaws of the powerful monster.

His father rushed to him and turned off the machine. Blood was everywhere. His jeans were splattered with the bright red liquid. But David felt nothing. He looked down in horrified shock to see his mangled arm. His father applied a tourniquet, carried him to the pickup truck and rushed to the family doctor. He was immediately transferred to a large nearby medical center. Within a few hours, David was undergoing surgery with a team of internationally recognized surgeons. David awakened the following morning to discover he was in a battle to save his arm, wrist, and remaining three fingers. His first response was to shout, "Cut it all off. I don't want a mangled limb that people will stare at. I've got plenty of guts. Just cut it all off!"

During the next three months David harvested a golden concept: hope for the future. As he talked with the hospital chaplain, his old feelings began to fade, and new vistas of courage unfolded. David, the young farmer, learned that courage was not walking unprepared into the face of danger. He had known the hazards of farm equipment, but he had thought of himself as brave enough to take a chance. Now he knew that taking a chance was not an expression of courage but of foolish unconcern. Visions of disregard for safety ran through David's mind as he thought about his friends back home. He wanted to tell his jean-age visitors to stop taking idiotic chances, to stop driving recklessly, to cease the experimental drinking and the flirting with the mind-blowing drugs. Yet David knew there was little chance that they would listen to him. Perhaps later they too would know that hope for the good life does not come from taking unnecessary chances.

David learned also that to give up and take the costly way out of suffering was not necessarily an expression of hope. He had cried out in agony for them to cut off his arm. But later he understood that it would take more courage to face the world as a changed person. His fears centered around being rejected by girls. Also, he feared the long and sometimes painful rehabilitation process. He did not at first realize that real courage would be facing both situations and not giving up. David thought of his friends again. He longed to tell them to take heart, to hang in there, and not to give up in a time of struggle. He thought of Sally who had mentioned quitting school. She had said, "I've got the guts to face the world without a degree—I don't care what people say." *How could he tell her about the courage to face school and have hope that she too could learn?* he thought to himself. He remembered a friend who had quit going to church because the pastor didn't relate well to teenagers. He mused, *How can I convince him to use his courage and hope to talk with the preacher to try to change things?* Recovery was a slow but certain process. David's body did heal more quickly than expected. The specialists were impressed with the way he faced the process of rebuilding and learning again to use his lower forearm, wrist, and hand. David did lose the battle to save several fingers, but he won the battle against despair. He found hope to carry a mangled stump with one finger and a thumb back into his hometown. He said, "It's strange, but I feel like a whole person in a new way."

David the farm boy had become David the young man in his battle to regain the use of his limb. David found that courage meant being willing to face the results of one's actions. "Don't give up just because something bad has happened to you," he told a girl at school who had gotten pregnant. She put the baby up for adoption, but she was afraid to go back to school. He explained to her that courage and hope meant continuing to work for the good and not to give up. For David, such hope was rooted in Christ's forgiveness and the belief that Jesus would walk by his side no matter what. Courage to face the future can only be based in a faith that God is at work in the world. David said, "I don't think God is sitting on a cloud, pulling strings, and making people behave like puppets. If that were so, why would God have pulled a string to put my arm in that awful machine? I did that because I forgot to turn off the machine."

Youth may or may not agree with David's reflections on courage and hope, and they may or may not understand his new sense of God's presence for facing the future. Nevertheless, this story can provide them with an opportunity to discuss faith and God as a source of strength and to examine their own sense of hope and groundedness in the face of tragedy.

After hearing teenagers' living stories and deciding that perhaps they do need further help, adults still face the task of convincing the youth. Building a bridge to the youth is difficult enough; building a bridge from the youth to a source of help can be a delicate matter. The following story has been useful with some teenagers. You may want to modify it and these other stories as you use them with the youth in your life.

How to Get Help

Do you ever feel so frustrated you can't decide what to do next? Every place you turn you seem to hit a brick wall, a dead end, or a blind alley? At times life feels like a giant chess game, and you're trapped in a corner. Every way out of the frustration looks blocked. Every passage to a better situation seems clogged. Every solution appears to bring even a bigger problem to be solved. What can you do when life seems to be at such an impasse? How do you get out of a teenage trap that's so frustrating? Well, there is some hope. Listen up. Do you ever feel so confused you can't decide to do anything? One friend tells you to do one thing, and another says just the opposite. Thoughts and ideas whirl through your head so fast you're dazzled, dazed, and downright rattled. Life seems to be a spinning merry-go-round that never stops.

Have you ever felt that you were stumbling through a fog in a strange neighborhood and couldn't see life clearly? Perhaps you wonder how you can find a sense of direction when life is so confusing. We'll discuss some ways of getting help in a moment.

At other times, you feel so helpless that you're frozen in place and can't move. It's as if life is a real game of freeze-tag. And all around you are problems stalking you like giants. You simply feel powerless, weak, unable to do anything to make things better.

At some other time you may feel like you are a small child on a playing field with angry, powerful giants. Your strength is drained, you can't do one more thing, and yet the giants continue to push and shove you around.

Have you ever been so upset and hurt that you wanted to just give up? Someone you love and trusted may have let you down, broken a promise, told a painful lie, or gotten themselves into trouble. You feel shocked, numb, and just can't believe that it's true. You may think to yourself, *Surely I'm dreaming. I'll wake up soon and realize that this is just a bad dream, a nightmare.* But it's not a bad dream, and the flood of painful emotions rush through your whole self like an angry river cutting a grand canyon through your heart. You think you'll never stop wanting to cry, or that if you cry you'll never stop crying.

If you ever feel overwhelmed by emotional pain, there is hope, and there is help. "Help?" you say. "How can I find help when life is so frustrating and so hopeless? Who knows what's going on in my life, and how could they ever understand the exact situation I face? There are no ways of getting out of this pain. There are no answers. Life is not going to change."

Step One: Realize You Need Help

There are some steps that youth can follow in getting help. The first step is realizing that you need help. Knowing that you are at wit's end is not difficult. You know when things are too heavy, when you are in over your head, when you don't know what to say. But you have to admit it and want help. Jesus once asked a man, "Do you want to be healed?" At first that may seem like a silly question to ask a sick person, but Jesus asked him to get the man to say he really wanted help. The I-can-do-it-by-myself attitude gets in the way of getting help. Perhaps you could help yourself a bit, but why go it alone and take the chance? What if you can't handle all of the pressure alone? Don't be too proud to ask for help. It's not a sign of failure or weakness—it's really a sign of maturity, wisdom, and strength. Although you may fear that others will ridicule, poke fun, and maybe even reject you if they know you're getting help, that's not really the case. They will respect you in the long run, so the first step in getting better is to decide that you need help and that you're willing to take the risk.

Step Two: Find Someone You Can Trust

Your second step in getting help is to find someone you can trust. Selecting the right person may not be easy. You don't want to select someone who is in as much trouble as you are; that will likely make matters worse. You may be reluctant to turn to someone you don't know, especially someone who is a stranger to your friends also. If a person you do not know offers help, don't grab him in desperation without checking him out. It might be a setup. Find someone that others have trusted, perhaps your parents, a relative, a teacher, a counselor, or a minister. Do reach out to one person and avoid telling your problems to too many people who aren't potential helpers. Gossip and misunderstanding might just add to your mess. Gossip certainly won't help anything. As you are looking for someone to help, the person you select may need to refer you to a professional. Ask for information about the professional and get to know the professional as a person yourself. If you are without any source of help, go into a hospital or a clinic or call the local crisis line, and they can help you in the process of finding someone you can trust.

Step Three: Be Open and Honest about Your Pain

The third step in really getting help is to be open and honest as you talk about your pain with the helping person. As clearly as possible, tell the helper the truth, share what you are feeling, and make your deeper needs known. In plain words, explain to the person why you feel the way you do. Don't beat around the bush—honesty is the best policy when you're looking for help. Sometimes you may have shameful, painful, unpleasant things that need to be shared. You may feel that it's even wrong to talk about them. If so, be as straightforward as possible and describe the situation without giving all of the information. Then trust your caring professional.

Step Four: Be Open to the Possibility of Change

Your fourth step in getting help is to be open to the possibility for change. Keep hoping that together you can make things better. This is not to say that your first choice of what's going to change will become reality. It may be that your choice is an unrealistic hope.

After you and your helping person talk about how you feel and your points of view, begin together to explore some alternatives. What are the possible things that you can do? What are some things you may need to stop doing? How will you implement these choices? Fantasize together about the future. Dream about the way life could be, and then plan to make it that way.

Some of your new ideas may be more work than you would like.

You may think that the way out is too much hassle. You must decide which is worse: your reason for getting help or the way out. It's difficult at this point to consider the long range. Of course, we all want immediate gratifications, but just talking with someone may not bring about immediate relief. Sure, it will bring some temporary relief, but in the long run you are going to have to do the growing and changing. And unless something is done, even the temporary good of getting things off your chest won't last long.

Step Five: Build Support for Your New Choices

Your fifth step in getting help is to build support for your new way of doing things. Find others who agree with your new choice. Let your parents, grandparents, and friends become a cheering section to urge you on when the going gets tough. They'll care about you, and they will want to see you grow. Having a few special people on your side makes changing easier. Burdens don't seem as heavy when someone is walking beside us to share the load. You don't have to go it alone.

Step Six: Evaluate What You Learned and Share It with Others

The sixth step in getting help is to decide what you have learned and then begin sharing it. You will know that you have really worked with a problem when you can help others work through the same problem. Try to give away what you have received: it will grow even more. As you help others, you will grow even more. You will discover the secret of being a "wounded healer." None of us is perfect, but if we let God use our imperfections, we have something to offer others.

Do you recall the story in the Bible about the man who was given the talent and then lost it because he refused to invest it for others? Your best resource for growth is to give away what you have gained, to share what you have gained with others, and help them grow.

Talking with teenagers means hearing their living stories, deciding if they are indeed at risk, and guiding them to the appropriate sources of help. This chapter has summarized a number of indicators that help is needed, such as age appropriateness, brutalization, change, duration, extensiveness, faith, groundedness, hope, and isolation. Your stories can reshape the writing of their story.

5

Family Stories

Teenagers are intricately connected to their families, including their extended families. Adolescents' identity arises primarily from their family's sense of values and orientation. Although teens are in the process of establishing independence from the family and differentiating their identity from the family, they are still tightly tied to the family process. For decades, social science researchers have highlighted the capacity to deal with crises as a major factor that differentiates strong families from dysfunctional families. Teenagers in difficulty long for some response from their parents, even though they may fear their parents' anger or suspect that their parents no longer love them.

A hostile gang member arrested during an inner-city break-in surprised the social worker assigned to his case with a special note. The note pleaded with the social worker to communicate to the youth's mother who was in an alcohol rehabilitation center that he still loved her and that he wanted to know she loved him. Regardless of the level of deterioration in the family relationships, most teenagers still desire family support in a crisis.

In a recent workshop with a group of youth, I mentioned that I was working on a book about how to talk with teenagers and how to utilize their stories in helping them. One teen shot back immediately, "If you're writing the book for parents, you ought to entitle it, 'How to Listen to Your Teenager.' We need to know," he continued, "that when trouble comes, our parents will hear us out completely and be on our side." The clear word for fathers and mothers is to communicate a willingness to stay by the teenager no matter what the crisis. When crises come, effective families work together toward the best possible outcomes. Ineffective families permit crises to tear them apart and destroy the family system.

Teachers, youth ministers, pastors, and other professionals who work with youth need to be aware of the power of family support in crisis resolution. In listening to adolescents tell their stories, one must be certain to understand the teenagers' family system. Begin with father and mother (and stepparents if they exist). Gather information not only about the teenagers' relationship to these persons, but their relationship to each other and a bit of the family history. I have found it helpful with adolescents to go ahead and do a genogram (see Wynn, 132-134, for a concise introduction to the use of Bowen's genograms in formal pastoral counseling), including grandparents and stepgrandparents. I gain as much information as I can about these persons and their relationship to the teenager. A seventeen-year-old wrote these lines to express her response to her grandfather's death. He died when she was fifteen.

Smoke Rings

My grandfather used to smoke cigarettes—just like the one that the man across the aisle was smoking. Long, thin, with a scent so strong that it could lift you off the floor. Even though I had been around them all of my life, I never got used to them. Something about that smell was malignant and foreign. It burned my eyes and made me cough. I remember him thin from the chemotherapy. His face was as pale as the hospital gown that he wore. His ribs protruded from his chest like the sun trying to push its way into the morning sky. He was *so* weak. Too weak to hug me good-bye, but not too weak to lift that wicked roll of tobacco. I saw him lay it in the ashtray, next to his bed, and breathe his last breath, thick with black smoke. That last breath was much like the ones that man across the aisle took for granted. I wanted so badly to put out that cigarette in his hospital room . . . but I didn't. Instead, I let it die, long and slow just like my grandfather.

Frequently, the information provides insight into the teenager's crisis. For example, in dealing with a fifteen-year-old young lady whose grief was so intense that she had stopped functioning at school, I discovered that her grandmother had been dysfunctional for three years since her grandfather's death. She told that the grandmother had locked herself into her little four-room house and had not even been out on the front porch since returning from her grandfather's funeral. The grandmother's grief complications provided useful insight in assisting the teenager to deal with her grief.

Family identity, the image a family has of itself and the image the family thinks the community has of it, exerts pressure on the teenager's identity. As I listen to teenagers tell their stories, I attempt to find a place to ask, "What does your family name stand for in your neighborhood or in your community?" Youth who have lived in a stable community for a number of years reflect a clearer sense of family identity than those who have moved from neighborhood to neighborhood on a regular basis. When teens are unable to articulate the community's sense of their family identity, at least hear their sense of what their family claims to stand for. For example, they might say, "Our family is the community helper. My parents are involved in a number of organizations to make our community better. Mom headed up an effort to organize a block watch for our area, and Dad has been a scout master for years." Or, they might say, "Our family is the troublemaker. Mom and Dad don't speak to any of our neighbors, and it was that way the last three places we lived." This sense of family identity provides insight into the adolescents' sense of the family being there for them in a time of crisis.

Qualities of Strong Families

Those who work with families would do well to engage in activities that strengthen family relationships, not only for the benefit of the youth but for the benefit of other social institutions as well, especially the church. Strong families provide a strong foundation for adolescent development, but they also provide strong communities and effective churches. As we reflect on the family stories of teenagers, there are five additional areas that deserve attention. These, along with the capacity to face a crisis creatively, surface in a number of studies as the qualities of strong families (Stinnett, 305-314).

Have a Strong Religious Orientation

Research on healthy families shows a positive correlation between commitment to one's religious beliefs and successful family relationships. Of course, there are some happy families who do not go to church regularly. But the research has indicated a positive relationship between strong religious ties and strong family ties. Persons assisting adolescents in crises need to understand the family's religious orientation and to find some basis for recommending a strengthening of that orientation. Encouraging spiritual development in the adolescents and their families can be an effective, although long-term, approach to helping both the teenager and the family. In strong families, religion plays a major role in the family's commitments and priorities.

In fact, a strong religious orientation and the capacity to deal with a crisis positively frequently go hand-in-hand. When adolescents sense their parents groundedness and feel the parents' commitment to them, they are themselves more oriented toward growth. A middle-aged pastor shared this story from ten years before when he had been in another church. One Sunday morning about 4:00 a.m. he received a phone call from the chief of police in their small town. "Pastor," he said, "we have your son, Danny, and two other boys at the police station. You need to come and pick them up. They ran a stop sign, and there was an open can of beer in the car. Danny was driving." After retrieving his son from the police headquarters, the pastor knew he must face his congregation in a couple of hours. The rumors had spread quickly, and everyone wondered what the pastor would say about the previous night's incident. Danny was sitting on the second row with his mother. The other two friends were with their parents. It had been several years since Danny had sat with his mother in church—he was accustomed to sitting in the balcony with his friends.

The pastor stood and told his congregation that undoubtedly they had heard of the previous night's incident involving his son, that he regretted the incident, and that he and his son apologized. But if the congregation doubted his ability to deal with his son, the pastor wanted them to know that he had only one son, and there were many churches where he could pastor. He assured them of his commitment to his son and his willingness to deal with the situation. The son was not in difficulty again. Several years after the incident, when the son had completed college and was working in the Department of Criminal Justice for the state, he shared with his father that the drinking incident really was not his doing. Although he had been in the car, he had not drunk any beer, and he was not driving. When the police pulled them over, he quickly slipped into the driver's seat and took the rap. "Why in the world would you have done that?" his father asked, puzzled. "Because, Dad, you see," Danny replied, "I knew that you and Mom would stand by me no matter what happened. And I wasn't sure at all what Tommy's dad would do to him."

Have a Commitment to Family

This story reflects another characteristic of strong families. Strong families have a commitment to each other and a commitment to the family unit. The old saying, "When the going gets tough, the tough get going," is certainly true in family crises where teenagers are involved. Teenagers who know their parents are committed to them and who are committed to their families get in less trouble in the first place; and in the second place, they are more likely to recover from a crisis if one does occur. Ephesians 5:21 is an excellent model of mutual commitment among family members. It reads, "Be subject to one another out of reverence for Christ." The rest of the chapter, verses 22-31, talks about marriage commitment. In chapter 6, verses 1-4 pick up the mutual commitment theme in relationship to parents and children. Paul did not surprise his audience with the first statement, that children are to obey their parents and to honor them as the first Commandment with promise. But, certainly, verse 4 must have been shocking in its first reading: "Fathers [parents], provoke not your children to wrath but bring them up in the nurture and admonition of the Lord" (KJV) You see, "Be subject to one another" calls for commitment not only from children to their parents, but also from parents to the children

Commitment was at the heart of Danny's understanding of his parents' willingness to stand by him. He knew they were committed to him!

Have Open, Effective Communication

Open, clear, and effective communication is the fourth characteristic of healthy families. Families where teenagers and their parents can talk openly and honestly about a variety of topics as well as share their deeper feelings and needs with each other are strong families. The ability to speak one's mind without fear of being reprimanded assists teenagers in communicating with their parents. When parents complain that their adolescent doesn't want to talk with them, you might ask the parents if the adolescent will be free to really say anything on his or her mind. If not, encourage the parents to open up the topics for communication.

Communicating thoughts, talking about places, people, and things is difficult enough for many teens and their parents, but communicating feelings can be even more intimidating. I found it helpful to encourage teenagers to use a fill-in-the-blank approach to beginning the communication process on an emotional level with their parents. I ask them to complete the following sentence: "I feel _____ toward _____ because _____, and I feel it this much: _____." For example, "I feel *warmly* toward *Mom* because *she takes me wherever I need to go*, and I feel it this much: *pretty much*. When adolescents can identify their feelings, claim them as their own, focus the cause and the direction of the feelings, and appropriately gauge the intensity, then parents can truly understand the communication. Some parents may also need to begin at the fill-in-the-blank level of communicating feelings with their teenagers. Communication workshops and exercises facilitate parent/adolescent dialogue.

Spend Time Together

Simply spending time together is another characteristic of strong families. This process is difficult to build if postponed until adolescence. One of my strange hobbies is making up "old Chinese" proverbs, like "He or she who does not play with their three-year-old will not have a thirteen-year-old around to play with." Spending time with one's teenagers usually is a result of having invested the time in one's children. Families who do not have a regular pattern of planned activities together can begin at a simple level of planning one activity a week. Strong families, however, work together, play together, eat together, worship together, and generally enjoy being together. One researcher found that strong families spend more time in outdoor activities together. Outdoor activities, such as camping and hiking, help a family experience a unique side of the world together.

Sometimes, unaware churches segregate adolescents and their parents and keep them from spending much time together. Whenever possible, retreats, fellowships, and family activities that can include parents and their teenagers reap long-term benefits.

Express Appreciation for One Another

The capacity to express honest appreciation one for another is a final characteristic of healthy families. Grady Nutt, a minister perhaps best known for his appearance on "Hee Haw," shared a game that he played regularly with his teenage sons. It was called "The Love Game." It simply consisted of each family member going around the room and saying to the other family members, "One thing I really love about you is . . . " and then sharing a positive compliment. For example, a teenage boy might say, "One thing I love about you, Dad, is the time you spend with me working on my car." "One thing I love about you, Mom, is the way you help me working on the computer." And perhaps even with some awkward stumbling he will be able to say to his sister, "One thing I love about you, Sis, is your enthusiasm and excitement about life." In the "Love Game," each family member must be taught to say "thank you" or in some way to express his or her gratitude for the compliment. Strong families not only give and receive appreciation, they share this appreciation with others when they are not in the presence of family members. I recently overheard a teenager say, "One thing I really like about my dad is the fact that I know I can trust him when he tells me something. Some kids, you know, don't believe their parents," he continued, "but I know my father's word is as good as gold."

Parents, assess your own relationship with your teenagers around these factors. How well do you deal with crises? How strong is your religious orientation? Is there a sense of commitment among your family members? Do you communicate clearly and openly? Do you spend quality time together? Is there an honest expression of appreciation between family members? You might want to talk with your teenagers and ask them to evaluate your family on all six of these areas. The conversation itself will be a good starting point for strengthening your family relationships. Now let us consider some family stories.

The following story is an example of how an ordinary incident can be turned into an opportunity for depth communication in a family context. Read this story and reflect upon your opportunities to discuss maturity with adolescents.

Marks of Maturity

A row of untidy pencil marks caught Chris's eye as he stood in the doorway of his grandfather's toolshed where he had taken refuge from a summer rainstorm. As he waited for the downpour to cease, he puzzled over those queer-looking lines. They were different lengths but placed all across the edge of the doorway. They began about three feet from the floor. The first ten or eleven were only a half inch or less apart. Then several were one or two inches apart. And there was one mark just above his head. He dashed into the farmhouse with the first break in the thunderstorm that had imprisoned him in the shed. "Papaw," he cried out, "what are those codes on the toolhouse door?"

His grandfather tried to make sense out of the question as they walked back toward the shed. But one look was all that it took to freshen Papaw's memory and solve the riddle. "Why son," Chris's grandfather began, "those are the marks that I made to show your dad how big he was getting when he was a boy. I used to measure him about every six months or so."

"What about that one?" Chris puzzled as he pointed to the long line just above his head.

"Humph," grunted Papaw. "I've never seen that one myself. We'll have to ask your dad."

Later Chris's father told of measuring himself on his sixteenth birthday to prove just how big he had grown. "I wanted Papaw to see that I was a real grown-up. But I never showed it to him," he continued hesitantly, "because later that day he and I got into a big argument, and I said some pretty childish things." Chris was surprised to hear his father talk about not feeling very grown-up and admitting that he had said some foolish things.

A few hours later, Chris was sitting on the front porch of the big farmhouse with his grandparents. He decided to ask them a question that had been bothering his fourteen-year-old mind since his father's confession. Chris screwed up all of his courage and said, "Papaw, how do I measure how grown-up I really am? I don't mean how tall I am, but how grown-up I am."

Chris and his grandparents talked for over an hour about that question. Chris had a physical picture of what it means to be grown-up. He talked about being tall and strong and fast, but beyond that he really had little to say. He mainly listened as his grandparents shared as if they were thinking out loud with each other.

His grandfather began by saying that one knew for sure he was a grown-up when he had his first full-time job. "A real part of being an adult is being your own provider," he said. "Of course, that doesn't happen all at once, but perhaps a fourteen-year-old can earn some of his own spending money. Usually a person must be eighteen or older to have a self-supporting job," Papaw concluded.

Chris's grandmother reflected that being a grown-up meant she could prepare a meal and help take care of the house. They all laughed when Chris piped in, "In that case, my dad still isn't very grown-up is he! He can't cook, and Mom still fusses at him to pick up his clothes."

Grandmother agreed that indeed his father still had some growing up to do in some areas, but then, "No one's perfect," she added. "At least grown-ups know how to take care of themselves. They may not always choose to do so," she concluded.

Chris asked if grown-ups got to be their own bosses and do as they please. Neither grandparent answered for a moment, then his grandfather began, "Well, yes and no."

Chris hated those middle-of-the-road answers. "What do you mean?" he inquired.

"Well, yes, grown-ups have a right to make up their own minds about things; they can vote for whomever they please, live wherever they choose, and all of that stuff," his grandfather said, "but real grown-ups do not make choices without thinking about the rights of others. They can't do just anything they want. There are responsibilities to be lived up to, so, no, they really can't always be their own bosses."

Suddenly the conversation got very serious, and Chris's grandmother surprised them all by talking about being grown-up in her heart. "Grown-ups take their feelings and the emotions of others very seriously," Grandmother said. "They know how to put off doing something fun even though they may not feel like it if there's real work to be done. They can compel themselves to do whatever seems to be best, even when it's not fun. A person knows that he or she is really grown-up when others' feelings can be a part of their decision making. A grown-up knows how and when to share anger, joy, love, sadness, and many other feelings." She continued by saying that for her a sign of a grown-up heart was when someone could talk about feelings with others and could listen to their feelings. It meant being able to say "I love you" without trying to act silly about it, or it meant admitting one's mistakes and owning up to the wrong that had been done. "That takes a real man," she said as she turned and pointed to Chris.

Next it was Grandfather's turn to get extra serious. He surprised Chris a bit also. "Two more things are important marks on how grown-up you are," he asserted in a somber tone. "How you treat the ladies, Son, and how they treat you is one, and I guess how you keep in touch with God is another." Grandpa didn't say much about that, just that a man is a grown-up when he treats women according to the way they're supposed to be treated. He meant being respectful, caring, and honest, but he added, "In this day and age, I'm not sure how some women want to be treated. I guess you have to ask them."

"Religious 'grown-upness' is hard to measure," said Papaw, "but I think it means a sense of knowing who God is and how God wants you to live. It means treating one another with the kind of love that you have for God." Chris waited for him to say more, but he didn't.

Chris ended the conversation by thanking them for the time. He was really surprised that they had talked so openly. "Growing up is sure a lot more complicated than I ever thought," Chris confessed.

"Well, a lot of people have been growing up for a lot of years,"

Papaw responded. "I bet you'll make it too."

Questions

Reflect on the elements of communication present in this story and evaluate your relationships with adolescents in light of it.

Can you discuss these and other topics openly with the teenagers in your world?

Do you share your own points of view, strengths, and weaknesses openly with teenagers?

Do you think Chris's parents could have had the conversation in the same way his grandparents did? Why or why not?

What would you add to the list of things that make a person grown-up if you had been talking to Chris?

Now consider a second story for use with youth. This story reflects appreciation and commitment between siblings. It has been used effectively as a discussion starter with teenagers so they can reflect on their relationships with their own brothers and sisters.

Sisters Are Forever . . . Brothers Are Too?

"You get all the breaks," griped Lynn. "You get your own room; you have a CD player and your own TV. You get the new dresses, and all I get are hand-me-downs. Now you've even got a car."

"Oh, shut up!" yelled Barb, Lynn's eighteen-year-old sister. "Get off my back and go count your pimples, or do something with that stringy hair of yours. Do anything, but stop complaining and whining like a baby. You sure don't act like a fourteen-year-old."

Lynn thought to herself, *I don't have to take that. I only have a few blemishes. She doesn't have to be so cruel. What if she is beautiful? I still deserve some of the breaks in this house.* Then in a flash, Lynn picked up her hairbrush and hurled it at Barb's turned back as she cried out, "I hate you, you big spoiled Daddy's girl!"

Barb turned to face Lynn, her back still throbbing from the blow. She raised her hand distinctly to slap Lynn as she had done on more than a few occasions, but her arm and hand froze in midair as she glimpsed Lynn's sorrowful brown eyes. Barb could hardly believe her own words as she said to her little sister, "It must really be tough being the little sister to someone like me. I guess I've been too busy growing up myself to notice what was happening to you. C'mon, sit down on the bed, and let's talk about it."

Lynn could hardly believe her ears, but she threw her arms around Barb's thin shoulders and sobbed for a moment. During the next two hours, they shared a long overdue sister-to-sister talk.

Things didn't work out quite so well for Ken and Miles. Ken, who had had his driver's license for less than a month, rubbed it in on his "little brother" who was fifteen but already two inches taller and much stronger. In a dash to the bathroom they had to share, Miles tripped Ken. Before Ken could get up, Miles locked the bathroom door behind him and jumped into the shower. Using a key that was stashed behind the hallway lamp, Ken entered the bathroom and started tossing cups of cold water over the shower door. Miles stormed out to get even, slipped on the wet tile, fell, and cut an ugly eight-stitch gash over his left eye.

Even after a stern lecture from their father, Miles and Ken were each blaming the other for the accident. Their sibling conflicts worsened over the next week. At times they went for days without even speaking to each other. Only after college separated them did they begin to appreciate each other at all.

Brothers and sisters do have their fights. Problems crop up in most homes that have two or more children. Siblings fear they are not getting their fair treatment. One can become jealous of the other's accomplishments, looks, honors, or just about anything. Conflict erupts from little but irritating, nerve-wracking, picky disagreements. I have known teenagers to hassle over a piece of cake, changing the TV program, doing chores, a bump as they passed in the hallway, or a forgotten phone message. Think about the following guidelines for helping teenage brothers and sisters get along. Do you agree these should be rules in most homes? Are they practiced in your home?

Guidelines for Siblings

1. *Treat siblings like you want to be treated.* Do unto others as you would have them do unto you and love your neighbors as yourself. This means at least being fair and giving as good as you get.

2. *Avoid trying to get even—two wrongs do not make a right.* The ability to call off a fight and resolve problems helped Barb and Lynn. Ken and Miles lacked that capacity.

3. *Try not to fuss and bicker.* Keep your temper. Blowing up over every little thing in life creates unnecessary conflict. You do not have to be a doormat and let your brothers and sisters walk on you, but patience will go a long way. After all, you are in the same family.

4. *Put yourself in their place, try to understand their feelings.* If you thought like they thought, would you feel the way they feel? Realizing that their feelings are based on how they see things will help you understand them. You may not see eye to eye, but at least you can understand their feelings.

5. *Respect each other's privacy.* If you have your own rooms, this means knocking before entering. If you share space, it means respecting their privacy and their space. It may just be a closet or a drawer or a shoe box that is their secret, private place, but respect it. Respecting privacy also means not listening in on each other's phone calls or reading each other's mail.

There are numerous other guidelines that can assist siblings when conflict erupts in their home. These rules will get you started on reducing the level of conflict and increasing your appreciation for each other. Add your own rules.

A third family story focuses on parent-youth conflict. The following story has been used as a participation story with a number of youth groups. After introducing the general topic of what makes parents act like we do, I suggest a few reasons and then ask the teenagers to suggest their own. The list is updated over the years.

What Makes Parents Act Like We Do?

"My parents don't understand me at all," moaned Julie. "My father expects me to be perfect. He thinks like a computer and wants me to agree with him on everything he says. I never know what my mom will say—she's so wishy-washy. One minute she's on my side, and the next minute she's on Dad's side. What makes parents act like they do anyway?"

Each of us would give different answers to Julie's question. Your parents might fit into some of the following reflections on why parents act like we do.

Language Barrier

Parents act like we do because we don't know how to speak your language. Parents want to communicate, but we have difficulty talking with you. We really don't stop to think about it; we have so much on our minds that we speak using our terms, our way of understanding, and our presuppositions. Most parents really want to know what's going on. It's just that listening to our children isn't a skill we have developed.

Memories of Own Mistakes

Parents act like we do because we remember our teen years and we want to keep you from making the mistakes we did and help you grow in some areas where we failed. Sometimes parents try too hard to make it easier. We try to make decisions for you. We assume that you are facing the same problems we did. We push you too hard, all in the name of not letting you make the same mistakes that we made. We forget that when we were teenagers we didn't always listen to adults who tried to do the same for us. We act like we do because we remember our own adolescent mistakes, and we are just trying to help.

Personal Frustrations

Another reason parents act like we do is that we have our own problems. We face frustrations at work, difficulties with neighbors, problems in the world at large, and conflicts with each other as parents. Oftentimes, the pressures that build up in our lives spill over into the way we treat you. We don't intend to do this; we just let the pressure pile up and lose control of it. Help us to understand when you think we are dumping on you.

Lack of Trust

Another thing that makes parents act like we do is we don't trust teenagers. We don't trust youth for several reasons. One, we watch too much television and see teenagers portrayed in a bad light. Two, we hear the stories of teenagers in difficulties. We read it in the newspapers. We permit ourselves to get a negative picture of youth in general. You can help us to trust teenagers by telling us good things about your friends. Bragging on what they do won't make us push you to live up to them so much as it will help us change our image of teenagers. Tell the good-news stories about today's youth, and your parents will begin to trust you(th) a little better.

Busy Schedules

Another reason parents act like we do is we are too busy. Most parents have too many activities. We're involved in work, church, trying to tend to the home, and a variety of other activities. Single parents are even busier. We overschedule our weekends and sometimes miss your special events. Let us know how important it is to be there. Stand up for yourself; remind us that we need to be there.

Different Values

Another reason parents act like we do is that we have a different drummer. Parents, more so than teenagers, tend to value economic security, getting ahead in the world, making something of ourselves, accumulating power, and having money. We forget that as teenagers you might appreciate these things, but you value excitement and newness; you value free time, and you still have an element of being like a little child. We forget that Jesus said unless we have the faith of a little child we will not know the kingdom of heaven. Please understand that we may worry too much; help us to be playful with you.

Ignorance of How to Love Teenagers

Another reason parents act like we do is we are not sure how to love a teenager. Oh, we know how to love a baby and protect it and cuddle it, how to coo, kiss, and hug it. We know how to love little children—we hold them and bounce them and laugh and play with them. But, we're not sure how to love a youth. We know you don't want us to hug and kiss you in public. We sometimes feel uncomfortable showing affection privately. When parents learn that we can love teenagers much the same way we love adults—respect them, support them, listen to them, and verbally say, "I love you"—then we relate a little better. You can help us in that area, teenagers. You can begin by sharing your love with your parents; maybe we'll learn.

What would you add to the list of what makes parents act like we do? Do you agree with the items on this list? What have teenagers told you about their parents that needs to be shared with other youth?

As we listen to the stories of adolescents, we will hear many family themes. Pay special attention to appreciation, time, religious orientation, communication, commitment, and dealing with crises. Evaluate the strengths and undergird activities that will increase the family's capacity to relate in these areas. As you tell your stories to teenagers, remember to listen to theirs; let the dialogue lead you and them to journey into areas unknown that you might find yourselves in new relationships.

Single Parents

Single parents, perhaps more than any other group of parents, feel the pressures of depleted time, drained emotional energy, and limited financial resources. Nine out of ten single-parent families are headed by the mother. Usually she is frustrated by the lack of adequate time to earn a living, care for the household, and respond to her teenage children's many needs. She feels emotionally drained because the demands for emotional output far exceed the opportunities for input. Because of the heavy responsibility of tending to her family, she likely has little time for her own social life or involvement with friends. Furthermore, research indicates that households headed by single mothers far exceed two-parent households in the percentage of income below the poverty line. As bad as the situation appears, it is aggravated and even worse during the first adjustment years following a divorce.

"How do I explain to my three teenagers why our family has fallen apart? Their father and I argued, but a lot of families argue. We perhaps were a little worse. I don't want to tell them about his girlfriend—I'm not sure when she entered the picture. She wasn't so much the cause of the divorce." Six months later, after the father had married the girlfriend who was only twenty-two herself, the children voiced their anger directly at their father. This resulted in a broken relationship with their refusing to visit with him for a number of months. The situation also created further stress on their mother. She had used the day the children were with their father as an opportunity for some personal time and replenishing of her emotional resources. Now she had no time for herself.

Single parents not only face more stress than two-parent families, frequently churches and other community agencies primarily program for the two-parent family. For example, family enrichment conferences often will omit single-parent issues for topics of discussion, or tack them on at the end. With one in three teenagers not living with both biological parents, programming needs must be altered.

The Scripture promises that if we train up children in the way they should go, they will not depart from it (Prov. 22:6). Single parents, like couples, reap the benefits or harvest the mistakes of the child's earlier training. However, they are not in an irreversible situation; they can still train an adolescent. The movie *Parenthood*, designed to show a variety of family mistakes, depicted a hassled, harried, frustrated, and overindulgent single mother. Her teenagers reflected a variety of problems—drugs, identity confusion, and pregnancy among them. However, as she fought, settled conflicts with them, and reached for her own integrity, her children began to respond and grow toward responsible adult behavior.

"Train up a child" is a good model for any age child. This does not say, "Tell children which way they should go," "Remind children which way they should go," or "Give the children a book about which way they should go." It does say *train*. Adolescents are best trained by the example of their parents. Perhaps the wisest choice for single-adult parents is to face a crisis in the way that would assist their teenagers to do likewise. If this means seeking additional counseling, then do so. Teenagers particularly imitate the behavior of the significant adults in their lives. Single parents who can close their eyes to some of the other pressures and focus on the need for relationship with their teenagers earn the respect of the teenagers, and they have an opportunity to mold these adolescent lives.

One single parent recently told of shopping on a very limited budget and being given twenty dollars too much change as she cashed her paycheck at the grocery store and paid for groceries. Her teenager was astonished that she quickly called the error to the clerk's attention and returned the twenty dollars. "Why, Mom," he protested, "we could have really used that money."

"I know," his mother said, "but honesty is honesty, and I just wouldn't feel right keeping that money."

A few weeks later the teenage boy came in very early from a Saturday night outing. "What's wrong, Tony?" his mother inquired.

"Oh, nothing, Mom," he replied.

"Why don't you tell me about it," she persisted.

"Well, it's just that some of the guys were going over to do some stuff that I didn't think was right. I told them I wasn't going along with it. And they said 'OK' and dropped me off at home. Mom, I don't know about some of my friends. They are going to push over mailboxes with the jeep. I guess what you said about honesty just sticks in my mind, and I can't get it out."

Teenagers do as we do, not as we say. While the pressures of being a single parent create an enormous burden, they can provide an opportunity for the parent to model living with integrity under stress and valuing relationships for the teenager. Surely the reader can look around and see numerous single parents of whom you are proud. Learn from those individuals. They are individuals who have made sacrifices and have steered their adolescent sons and daughters toward responsible adulthood by being examples of right living.

Of course, the opposite is also true. Teenagers will copy negative behavior. A single mother brought her daughter to me for counseling with a can-you-fix-her? attitude. On the phone the mother had said that the daughter had been caught smoking pot at school, gotten three speeding tickets in the first two months she had her driver's license, and she feared the girl was "sleeping around" with her new boyfriend. After I talked to the teenaged girl, she admitted that she had had some difficulties, but she was not sleeping with her boyfriend. Then she added, "It wouldn't be any of Mom's business if I did."

"What do you mean by that?" I inquired.

"Well, you see, Mom lets her boyfriend spend the weekends every time I'm over at Dad's. I don't see that it makes any difference." She went on to explain that her mother regularly used a "fuzz buster" to speed on the interstate when they were driving to see the grandparents and that the mother and her boyfriend sometimes smoked pot themselves at parties. Later when confronted, the mother's defense was, "But I'm old enough to do these things, and she's not." How wrong of the mother. One is never old enough to violate the laws of the land and the commandments of the Scripture. Also, Paul told us that although it might be permissible to eat meat, he would not eat meat sacrificed to idols because he did not want to lead another astray or to offend another. Often, parents can be stumbling blocks to their own children.

Stepparents

Not infrequently single parents fantasize that remarriage will bring family wholeness and that their new spouse can relieve parenting responsibilities with their adolescents. Stepparenting, however, is a very mixed situation that can have many blessings but brings definite pressures and problems.

"I really like my new daddy," confided a thirteen-year-old whose mother had been remarried only two months. "Yes," she said, "he spends time helping me do my homework, buys me things, and he treats Mom so nice. In fact, they are sometimes embarrassing. They don't fight like Mom and Dad used to do all the time. He's nice," she mused.

"My stepfather is a crazy man," shouted Kent.

"What do you mean?" I inquired.

"He yells at me. The other day he shoved me when I told him he couldn't make me clean up my room. He told me that I would soon learn who was boss in this house. Well, I showed him. I'm going to live with Dad. I'm not going to put up with that stuff," he continued, exasperated.

The two adolescents were referring to the same man. Their experiences with their mother's new husband were radically different. Perhaps there are a number of reasons why. Upon reflection, a few of them had to do with the approach of the parents and the needs of the adolescent. The stepfather wanted to be a father to his stepchildren and while he could see the needs of a thirteen-year-old for attention, caring, and structure, he only saw the need of the fifteen-year-old to have some limits and discipline. He did not earn a relationship with the fifteen-year-old boy, but he attempted to take the role of father by force. His intimidating style only served to push the boy further away. The need of the fifteen-year-old for understanding and friendship was not as readily noticeable but nonetheless present.

Typical problems facing stepparent families involve discipline, dealing with sex roles, conflicting parent roles, sibling rivalry, and many others. When correcting children, it is usually better for the biological parent to handle the chastisement instead of the stepparent. The discipline needs to be consistent, clear, and in the context of emotional stability not irrational, angry outbursts.

While sexual abuse is more often a fear than a reality for stepchildren, having a "strange man in the house" can produce anxiety for adolescent girls. Stepfathers need to be controlled in their expressions of warmth toward stepdaughters, let physical expressions of warmth be paced by the stepdaughter's needs, and always in front of the other parent or some adult.

Adolescents whose biological parents are both living can be confused when the stepparent attempts to develop a parenting role. "I have one father," Kent complained later. "I don't need Mom's new husband trying to be my father too." The fourteen-year-old in the family mentioned earlier really rebelled when her father married the twenty-two-year-old. "I don't need two mothers—certainly not one who's almost my age," she complained. Stepparents are well advised to try to find a new role as stepparent and not attempt to replace the role of parent for the teenager.

Their new role as stepparent can best be characterized by an earned friendship that comes naturally over time from sharing activities and taking an interest in the teenager. This earned relationship does involve some confrontation and discipline, but it is more in the form of advice giving and statements about one's choices in life. For example, rather than assertively demanding, "Don't do that," a stepparent might say, "That hasn't worked well for me. Can we talk about it?" Stepparents need to know that building this new relationship with teenagers will take time. Patience, hope, and cautious warmth will win out in the long run.

If both parents in a blended family bring children into the situation, sibling rivalry looms to the forefront as a pressure. When sixteen-year-old Stacy learned that her mother was marrying Robert, she was frustrated. She became infuriated, however, when she learned that Robert had a sixteen-year-old daughter named Terri. Terri, although not as attractive as Stacy, had closets full of clothes, a late-model sports car, and was with the in-group at their high school. The friction between the two girls continued for over a year until it erupted one day in a physical fight. After several months of counseling as a family, the girls learned to respect each other's differentness, to share some of their similarities; and although they did not become good friends, they could be civil to each other. Perhaps more importantly, the parents learned the value of consistent treatment. They decided that both girls would receive similar cars, allowance, responsibilities, and freedoms.

Single parents, stepparents, blended families, and intact families all have their stories to tell. As you hear the stories of adolescents and their families, be aware that no two are identical and listen patiently for the differences. Perhaps Moses is the best Old Testament example of the success of a stepfamily. Remember that Moses, placed in a basket by his mother and hidden, as a child lived in two homes: that of his biological family and the home of the Pharaoh. While Moses was certainly influenced by living in Pharaoh's palace, it was the loving care of a family that ultimately shaped his identity.

Having considered family stories, we turn our attention to another major concern: peer relationships. Friendship stories will guide us in our understanding of coping with adolescent peer pressures.

6

Friendship Stories

"The soul of Jonathan was knit with the soul of David" (2 Sam. 18:1, KJV). Thus begins the description of perhaps the most famous teenage friendship in the Old Testament. Jonathan, son of King Saul, observed David, son of a peasant farmer, defeat the giant Philistine Goliath. Jonathan's friendship with David remained firm over the years even when Jonathan's father set in his mind to kill David.

Few adolescents are fortunate enough to have a soul-mate friend like Jonathan. Nevertheless, they long for just such a relationship. Teenage friendships develop over a period of time. The widespread mobility in American culture breaks up many such friendships before they have an opportunity to form. Perhaps less than 5 percent of American adolescents are friends with persons they knew during their preschool years. Friendships change rapidly for most teenagers, and the capacity to make new friends is essential for overcoming loneliness. As the nature of youth's friendships unfolds in this chapter, attention will focus on the influence of cultural factors on peer groups, the levels of friendship, the levels of dating, and living legends among the youth. Youth who are fortunate enough to maintain friendships with one or more adults find extra strength for their journey from childhood into adulthood.

Positive Functions of Peer Groups

Contrary to the belief of some parents and youth workers, peer groups do serve a variety of positive functions in the adolescent's development. The peer group receives more blame for unruly behavior than is justified. Projecting on to the peer group does relieve families from self-incrimination when their youth get into difficulty. Granted, peer groups do contribute to negative behavior, but the family has its responsibility also. Peer groups and friends assist teenagers by informing them on numerous subjects, encouraging them in a variety of settings, reinforcing their identity in many areas, setting limits on their behavior in different situations, engaging them in fun in an array of activities, and encouraging them toward independence as individuals.

Peers Learn from Each Other

Youth learn as much from each other as they do in formal education. Of course, they learn different things. Formal education provides teens with knowledge on a number of important subjects. The peer group provides youth with knowledge about life itself. When I asked teenagers where they get most of their information about dating, sex, money, how to find a job, and other such significant topics, the unanimous response is "from my friends." While not all information would be trustworthy and accurate, the peer socialization process adds much in a positive sense to the task of growing up.

Peers Encourage Each Other

Encouragement from friends motivates teenagers in the right direction. "C'mon, you can do it—give it your best shot" represents a cheer from the sideline during an athletic event as well as the words of a friend during study for an examination, practicing for a driver's license test, or preparation to enter a rehabilitation program. Having friends pull for them builds confidence and creates the hope necessary to overcome difficulties. "I knew I would have to make the best of it," said a young man recovering from an automobile accident. "So many of my friends were pulling for me that I couldn't give up."

Peers Reinforce Each Other's Identity

Friends serve as mirrors to reinforce each other's identity. Youth frequently turn to hairstyles, clothing, "in" language, and personal mannerisms that reflect uniformity. The need to belong is so strong that imitating one another reinforces a sense of acceptable selfhood. While there is a danger that a few youth might slip into conceit and egocentric pride, the larger portion need the identity reinforcement from friends in order to have a healthy sense of acceptance of who they are. The communal sense of identity formation, ritualized in more primitive societies, often gets neglected in contemporary society. Perhaps receiving a driver's license, being inducted into an honorary society, playing on an athletic team, or performing with a musical group could be considered modern, middle-class rituals that reinforce the identity. They certainly lack the sense of universal cultural reinforcement. Most teenagers are left to their own ingenuity in finding ways to identify with the group and thus shore up their identity.

The authority of the peer group, especially for middle and older adolescents, overrules the power of parents, particularly when the parents are not present. While that authority might be feared by some adults, one must recognize that it is exactly this authority that sets limits on the behavior of most teenagers. Whatever the code of ethics of a given friendship circle, peer group, or teenage gang, the collective power of the group serves to enforce that code of ethics and thus sets limits on the behavior of the youth. Few teenagers dare violate the rules in their own peer group. One of the best methods of transforming a youth culture is to have an alternative youth culture whose membership is more highly valued and whose code of ethics is more respected.

Peers Participate in Fun Activities

"Boring, boring, boring, boring," echoes the chorus of teenagers heckling any activity that fails to live up to their expectations for excitement. Time moves so quickly for teenagers that adolescence could easily be called "a decade of living life in the fast lane." Teenagers need recreational opportunities to physically, emotionally, and mentally work off anxiety. The peer group serves the primary focus for having fun. Adolescents need opportunities for amusement, relaxation, and frolicking. If healthy opportunities for such pleasures do not exist, they will turn to pranks, antics, and tomfoolery that can lead to tragedy. Many a practical joke has ended in a personal crisis when fun seeking went undisciplined. Adults have a responsibility to see that adequate recreational opportunities exist for youth.

Peers Encourage Independence

The peer group serves as a halfway house between dependence on one's parents and personal independence. Friends serve a bridge function between childhood ties to the family and young adult freedom and individuation. Friends provide a place to be away from one's parents emotionally, as well as physically, and as such assist growing teens through the separation anxiety of leaving home and breaking the apron strings. Parents, youth leaders, teachers, and counselors who work with adolescents do well when they provide structured opportunities for youth to experience long periods of time with their friends. Overnight trips, slumber parties, and travel opportunities with friends add to the potential for constructive development of independence on the part of the teenager. Parents overly anxious about their youth's independence need to realize that independence is but a step toward adult-to-adult friendship between them and their adolescents.

While adults understand that friendships serve a positive function, youth only know that they long to have a friend. Frequently, when given the opportunity to ask questions in an unstructured setting, teenagers will inquire as to how to make a friend. They complain about being lonely, isolated, or even ostracized. It is not only the new kid on the block who feels unwelcomed in a social group; teenagers who have lived in a stable neighborhood still complain that friends have shut the door on them after they themselves have been accepted into a clique, or their friends have turned their backs on them now that they no longer share a common interest. For whatever reasons, adolescents long to know how to make new friends. In a recent workshop, the following suggestions were given by teenagers for helping other youth make and keep good friends.

- If you want a good friend, be a good friend.
- I make most of my friends while doing things we enjoy together. I have friends who play soccer, friends at church, and friends in the choir.
- If somebody's going to be your friend, you've got to treat that person like he or she is as good as you are. I mean, friends have to be equals with each other, kind of like "I'm OK, you're OK."

- If you want to keep friends, don't go around putting them down all the time. Friends have to know how not to fight too much, how to say nice things to each other.
- I think if you want friends, you have to let them know who you are. Opening up yourself to your friends and then listening to them tell about themselves is really important.
- People who want friends can't go around getting mad and going home. I know some guys who don't have any friends because they are always getting mad and quitting.
- If you want new friends, don't try too hard. Friendship is something that kind of happens while you're doing stuff together.
- If you want other people to like you, you've got to like yourself. You can't expect anybody to like you when you don't.

A lot of wisdom resides in the suggestions of those youth. In their own way they talked about the give and take of relationships, equality and respect for other persons, self-respect, and self-esteem as vital ingredients of youth friendships. Elements of flexibility, vulnerability, and involvement outside of oneself also are reflected.

As we listen to teenagers inquire about peer groups and making friends, we are wise to remind them of the New Testament concept of a caring community. The ultimate community is built on our common kinship as children of the one true and living God. As sons and daughters of a good and gracious God, we are called to live in relationship with one another in a way that will demonstrate self-giving love.

Impact of Social Change

The influence of cultural and social change on teenage peer groups has been subtle but staggering. The counterculture revolution of the 1960s and early 1970s and the polarization of society in the 1980s has replaced the pathway to social acceptance with a multidimensional maze leading in many directions. A generation or two ago teens could count on social acceptance through one of several basic pathways. For some, academic, athletic, or musical talents led to social acceptance and positive peer support. However, such is no longer the case. Students who may at one time have been respected for their academic abilities are now referred to derogatorily as nerds, geeks, and brains. Students who at one time could expect to find acceptance through athletic accomplishments are now discounted and called jocks. Youth for whom music was the road to acceptance now may be discredited by the terms *wimp* or *punk*. Cliques have proliferated in most schools as a result of society's fragmentation itself. Even children of community leaders can no longer expect automatic acceptance.

Other social changes have left their mark. Movies, television, and magazines have so romanticized dating relationships that an unreal fantasy world is lived out by the few "pretty people" who do date while the remainder of today's adolescents struggle to find a sense of acceptance. Probably 15 to 20 percent of the seventeen-, eighteen-, and nineteen-year-olds date on a regular basis. The others feel left out and pushed aside. It seems that more adolescent girls than boys complain of the lack of dating relationships, but group dating and attending activities with friends have replaced individual dating for a large portion of American teenagers. Thirteen-year-old Rodney Culpepper expressed his feeling in the following poem:

> I dedicate this poem
> To the girl it's about,
> The girl in my life
> That makes me pout.
>
> For she's the type of girl
> That pushes me around,
> Then treats me like
> a baby hound.
>
> But when I see
> her cute little smile,
> I have to stop
> and think a while.
>
> And try to remember
> What my name was, so
> When she asks me,
> I will know.

Not only is there a wide variety of cliques and increased pressure on dating, the current adolescent population also faces the expectation that they will get rich and have possessions. Parents are as guilty as anyone in pushing teenagers to see success not in terms of relationships, personal integrity, and developing one's natural gifts but rather in terms of getting to the top of some ladder. In a recent parent-youth dialogue, a member of a church shocked me with his reply to a teenage boy in the group. The teenager, who was obviously struggling with his own values in life, asked why he should be expected to go to church. Before anyone else could answer, the man jumped to his feet and said, "I'd like to answer that. Son, did you see that new car I drove into the parking lot? Look at this," he said as his thumb stroked a large diamond on his index finger. "And you know the kind of house we live in. That's why I go to church—to get ahead," said the member, unaware of his own sinful pride and misdirected values.

As already mentioned, the mobility of society isolates teenagers from their early childhood friends. It is not unusual for adolescents to have attended schools in four or more communities by the time they reach the twelfth grade. Forced termination from one's peer group creates grief. When the grief goes unaddressed, the adolescent chooses isolation rather than involvement with the new group. While a few self-confident youth can move frequently and maintain friendships in each new place, most do not.

The elevation of the sarcastic put-down to a level of affirmed brilliance has further alienated teenagers from one another. Witticisms, while sometimes cute, most often create hurt and rejection. Humor does not laugh *at* someone but *with* someone.

Situation comedies have so elevated cuts, put-downs, and insults that many teens imitate them and expect to be popular like the stars they see on television. They are surprised to learn that although their taunts, sneers, and innuendos bring some laughter, ooh's, and aah's from bystanders, they bring reproachment and ostracism from the victims. What may seem cute on television is so painful in real life as to devastate peers. Teenagers should not overpraise one another with puffy flattery and empty adulation, but as true friends they do need to give and receive honest affirmation. They can express disapproval privately without embarrassing one another.

A final factor that further serves to isolate adolescents from one another is the early age at which they are pushed into activities and driven toward success. As David Elkind so aptly argues in his book *The Hurried Child*, children who are pushed toward success too soon develop much anxiety. I recall counseling with a fifteen-year-old who had no close friends. From the age of six, he had practiced his violin three to four hours a day while other children were playing with each other. He was an accomplished violinist, but the personal sacrifices seemed too large in his mind. Ideally, youth would be able to pursue an activity and have balanced time for peer group activities.

Numerous other factors have impacted the deterioration of positive adolescent peer groups. Stories of loneliness and isolation abound. As we work together to build a user-friendly society for our youth, we need to be aware that they will not move from isolation to social integration overnight. Our churches need to be social "safe places" where youth can hide from the pain of rejection and find nourishment for their emerging identities. Many of them make the mistake of idolizing a particularly popular peer and feeling that they must reach that point of social acceptance to be personally satisfied.

Living Legends

Teens idealize certain peers and enhance stories based on half-truths to create "living legends" in their own peer groups. Youth put a premium on success and unique abilities. A living legend might be a sports hero who could dunk the ball in eighth grade or who scored a zillion points against an opponent or who has never been scored upon as a goalie. The living legend might be musically talented and playing with a rock band at a young age. Occasionally, a living legend is academically gifted and reported to have scored a perfect score on college entrance exams. A living legend might be a particular beauty queen or a tough gang member or a politically astute individual who has outsmarted the teachers and the adult system. While living legends inspire some teenagers, most are depressed as they compare themselves unfavorably with their idealized opponents. As you listen to stories of living legends, help teenagers evaluate the authenticity of the stories, appropriately judge the impact of the stories, realistically understand the nature of the person in the story, and, finally, help them to value their own giftedness and personhood. As we guide teens to evaluate the authenticity of the story, there are some basic questions they need to ask—not the least of which is, Where did we get the facts? Another is, Do we have the data to substantiate the living-legend nature of this story? Most likely there has been some jumping to conclusions and magnifying of the reality of the situation. David Burns, in *Feeling Good*, asserts that these and other cognitive distortions lead individuals to overreact emotionally and often feel depressed (p. 40).

Going back to get the exact news story or talking to the individuals themselves can assist in demythologizing the living legend. Of course, teenagers are going to feel put-down and rejected if they are comparing themselves to an inflated ideal.

To help a teenager judge the impact of the story, one needs to ask "So what?" If someone scores a perfect score on the college entrance exam, he or she still has to go to college and study and work. If someone is talented athletically, he or she still has the responsibility to use that talent. And even if the person is the best in the world and wins an Olympic gold medal, in a couple of years someone will come along and defeat him or her. Putting a living legend in context helps teens cope with their own inadequacies compared to the living legend.

If teenagers can realistically visualize the person behind the living legend, then they may even be able to imagine being a friend to that person. Research has indicated that a number of successful adolescents about whom living legends are written report themselves to be lonely, isolated, and frustrated. Beauty queens complain that persons want to date them in their roles as beauty queens but have no interest in getting to know them as persons. One young man who received "Athlete of the Year" at his high school confided in me that he was frustrated that other youth didn't want to talk to him about regular things such as music and studies, but they only wanted to relate to him around his athletic accomplishments. The same is true of other high school heroes. Youth who can focus on the personhood of a hero can be friends with that person.

A fourth way in helping teenagers deal with the living legends is to help them to value their own gifts. It is crucial to understand, develop, and accentuate their own sense of giftedness. At times I have retold living-legend stories inserting the adolescent with whom I am talking as the hero. As I overgeneralize and exaggerate at a few points, teens begin to see how they could be seen by others as a living legend. Deliberately magnifying their talents, abilities, or uniqueness will often bring smiles and laughter as they half jokingly denounce any right to be cast in the role of a living legend. The value of visualizing themselves as supercompetent is not so much to stroke their egos as it is to see that they must accept responsibility for themselves. They might continue to feel beneath the living legends in their social group; however, they are not likely to distort as much and thus visualize themselves as totally on the bottom. As they rethink their own situation, hope continues to grow.

Confronting living legends and dealing with the misconceptions will not automatically place teenagers in the in-group of their social system. However, teenagers who are constantly competing with persons they view as above themselves relegate themselves to frustration and failure. Ultimately, satisfaction comes in finding a few friends with whom they can identify and focusing on the relationship they have with other friends. When a teenager who has felt left out has a sense of belonging to a new group that really cares, that new group takes on living-legend proportions. They are heroes because they have dared to include him or her in their group.

Another common distortion among adolescents is that all other teenagers, except themselves, have many personal friends. In reality, there are levels of friendship like concentric circles, and while the numbers may differ, most youth have friends at each of these levels.

Levels of Friendship

A major ministry with youth is the ministry of introduction. An adult who knows of a common interest between two youth, and can introduce them to each other, serves an important function not only for the youth but in the youth group as well. Of course, introducing teenagers to potential dates and boy/girl relationships can be quite dangerous. But introducing friends is often productive. Adults who can go a step further and invite several youth into their home in order to meet a lonely teen provide an invaluable ministry.

Friend can describe a variety of relationships among adolescents. A disparity exists, however, in the way the term is used by thirteen- and fourteen-year-olds as opposed to its utilization among eighteen- and nineteen-year-olds. Understanding the various levels of friendship helps those who care for teenagers make an accurate assessment of the nature of their support system and establish goals for strengthening that nurturing group of peers.

The first level of friendship, common association, refers to basically being in the same place at the same time doing the same things on a regular basis. School friends who have an amicable relationship at school but no contact outside of school represent this first level of friendship. Such friends may share work assignments, choose each other as partners in lab, and even eat together at lunch. But the association is limited to structured activities. While such affiliations provide a limited measure of support for youth, they by no means can be counted on for sustaining energy during a time of crisis. Such relationships usually shift quickly with the reassignment of tasks or the changing of class schedules.

Phone friends and pen pals represent an increased level of friendship. Youth who not only share activities in a structured setting but also spend time communicating through the phone or in letters become more closely bonded to one another. The phone represents a safe but intimate method of communication. One can talk on the phone and have a person right at his or her ear and in private. The phone and written communication between friends provide a degree of safety as well as connectedness. Such friends may have seen each other at school but want to talk on the phone for hours on the same day. This is partially to pass time; it is also a way of being intimate without taking risks. Perhaps they could not share as openly face-to-face.

Phone friends can develop into a deeper level of friendship—social friends. Social friends belong to the same cliques, frequently sit together, spend free time together, and attend activities together. These friends represent more durable sources of support during a time of crisis than affiliations and phone friends would represent. There is a degree of instability in the cliques—often characterized by competitiveness for leadership and/or attention. Such subgroups may be the source of extreme frustration as a member becomes ostracized or when members begin to like the same member of the opposite sex. Friendships can deteriorate rapidly in a young love triangle.

The highest level of adolescent friendship, personal friend, was described by Jonathan as the "soul mate" of David. In a crisis, personal friends stand by one another. They not only share common activities, intimate conversations, and friendships, they go out of their way to make time to be together. They hang around together, doing nothing in particular. Being together becomes more important than the activity itself. They respect each other's dating relationships and would not think of dating each other's boyfriend or girlfriend. Close, personal friends at the older teenage level frequently value their friendship more than their kinship ties. When push comes to shove, if parents try to forcefully split up close friends, the peers will choose one another and reject their parents. This was the case with Jonathan as he turned against Saul, his own father, in order to protect his friend David.

Adolescents who are fortunate enough to have one or two personal friends can count on the friends in a time of crisis; and they receive much-needed support for self-confidence and encouragement from the relationship. Most such close, personal friendships are between youth of the same sex. However, occasionally, deep friendships are sustained between boys and girls who do not date each other. They might describe their relationship as brother-sister and be appalled at the thought of romance. In fact, if one of them does become romantically inclined toward the other, it is likely to end the friendship. Occasionally, both become romantically inclined at the same time, however, and the friendship can grow toward a mature love relationship.

Levels of Dating

Just as there are levels of friendship, there are levels of dating among adolescents. In traditional terms of a boy asking a girl for a date, going to her home and escorting her to an activity and returning her to her home, a small percentage of American teenagers would be considered dating. While many long for this type of relationship, few find it. The first level of dating is actually not dating but desiring to do so and being unable to sustain such a relationship. I refer to it as the "griping" level of dating. More females gripe because they do not have a boyfriend, although a growing number of adolescent males complain at their inability to find a suitable date. Both groups are usually idealizing themselves or romanticizing the dating scene and projecting that they will date some perfect person. All others pale in comparison to these projections. Therefore, their dating remains at the griping level, not the actual encounter with a human person.

Group dating is the second level of dating among teenagers. Informally this occurs when clusters of boys and girls attend the same function and interact on a regular basis, such as a church youth group going bowling together. On a more formal basis, group dating might be three guys and three girls going together to a school party, or it might be two guys and four girls going to a movie together and planning to get a pizza afterwards. While they enjoy each other's company, they are aware that such dating is not couple oriented.

The third level of dating—individual, casual dating—is sometimes fun and social togetherness. Most often, dating around is characterized by insincerity and game playing. (See the story following this section for an example of manipulative game playing in dating relationships.) A hierarchy exists in most social groups with boys wanting to date girls higher up the dating ladder than themselves and girls hoping to do the same. Surface issues tend to differentiate one's position on the dating ladder. Economic wealth, beauty, and popularity tend to overshadow honesty, personal integrity, and capacity for durability in a relationship. Frequently, such persons will point to factors like "We like the same rock groups" or "We're both football fans" or "We love Spanish" as the backbone of their relationship.

A fourth level of dating—going together—represents a commitment between a boy and a girl to date each other rather exclusively. A wide variety of terms such as *going steady, lavaliered, pinned,* and so forth refer to such relationships. If teenagers begin such a committed relationship too early, say thirteen or fourteen, they miss the opportunities for social development and may have difficulty in dating relationships later on. For older adolescents, such commitment is to be taken quite seriously and may result in a marriage. When such relationships are terminated, the grief can be near that of a divorce for adults and frequently leads to serious depression.

Dating Games

Teenagers have noted a number of complaints about dates. The following incidents can be shared with adolescents in a way that permits them to discuss their own friendship and dating relationships and to assess their level of maturity. As with the other stories, you will want to modify them for your particular context.

"If it weren't for you" is a game that dumps the blame for unpleasant situations on the other person. It begins with a complaint about something. When other persons attempt to comfort us, we turn on them as being the supposed cause of the suffering. As a result, they feel bad, perhaps even guilty; we feel relieved. Krista said to her date: "That movie was dull and boring. I wish I had not wasted my time watching it." He sheepishly responded: "I invited you because I thought you liked movies about swimming. I was just trying to be nice." Krista stabbed back by saying, "How could you possibly think I would like such a movie? If it weren't for you, we would have been having a fun evening." Krista's date felt hurt, rejected, put down. He didn't understand the set-up and her maneuvering in the dating game.

"If you loved me, then you would" is another dangerous game. This dating game is played to manipulate others into going along with whatever you want to do. The game usually begins with something like, "If you really loved me, you'd do it for me. You'd break that rule." The surprise comes when they do not stay by the other partners if they get in trouble. The "If-you-love-me" players abandon the other persons and leave them to face the failure, receive the judgment, pay the price, or reap the unpleasant consequences of whatever transpires. The first step in dodging this game is to be able to say, "And if you loved me, then you wouldn't pressure me."

Playing games on dates creates serious problems. Perhaps the most difficult game, first identified by Eric Berne as "rappo" in his book *Games People Play*, is one that I call "C'mon and try me." The game begins when someone flirts with another and then rejects that person with a put-down when the person responds to the flirtation. A girl might wink and smile at a boy. When he asks her to dance, she might rudely refuse him with "What makes you think I would dance with you?" Her payoff comes from "having to beat the boys off"; he feels rejected, and she feels elevated. One response to such a game is not to go over in the first place. But if the game is already in progress, it can sometimes be interrupted by "Your smile is what made me think you would want to dance with me. I'm sorry if I misunderstood."

Adult Friendships

Understanding the nature of adolescent friendships is essential in ministering to teenagers as they develop. It is even more important in responding to their emergencies and crises. Adolescents who are fortunate enough to have adult friends have an even stronger basis of support in times of crisis. A variety of friends enriches all persons' lives, but a variety of relationships for an adolescent is especially important. I like to use the metaphor of a bouquet of friends with teenagers. A bouquet has foliage, flowers, and just plain filler. Even a cocklebur, a thistle, or a bramble can be beautiful in the proper context of a bouquet. I frequently ask teenagers to list their friends who are under age twelve, over age twenty, over age forty, and over age sixty. I also urge teenagers to have friends who might be handicapped, of another ethnic group, or of another socioeconomic level from their own. Such friends not only provide a diversity of perspectives, but they also enrich the adolescent's appreciation for differentness.

Adults who can befriend youth can be their advocates at school, church, in the business community, or in a time of crisis. Such adults can also serve as an external authority in reinforcing appropriate values for the teenager. In a rather heated argument with her mother, a seventeen-year-old girl shouted, "Mrs. White would certainly understand my point of view! She would let her daughter do such a thing." The mother creatively called the daughter's bluff and said, "Let's call Mrs. White." "OK," said the daughter. "Let's go over and tell her our story." Mrs. White patiently heard both the mother's and the daughter's sides of the conflict. And then much to the daughter's surprise, she said, "I'm afraid I have to agree with your mother in this case." Because Mrs. White was a valued friend, the girl laughed, thanked her, hugged her mother, and declared the end of the conflict. Not all stories have such a happy ending, but adult friends can be a valuable ally for adolescents and their families.

Story: The Shadow of a Friend

"My boyfriend is just not a troublemaker. He got caught with the wrong crowd," cried Heather. "He did enjoy his fun, but he never intended to hurt anyone. He never should have gone with those Smith boys. They were the ones who hit that old drunk. David just helped them get away when the cops came," she continued.

Heather's friend had been arrested for aiding the getaway of three young men who were taking money from an elderly drunk on the street. The drunk tried to fight back, and one of them hit him in the back of the neck. He was hospitalized, in a coma. Heather could not believe her boyfriend had been involved in a robbery and an assault. After all, he was a good boy. She admitted that he enjoyed having a good time, and maybe he did get a little rough at times. He even bragged about a few close calls with the law, but she couldn't believe he was such an evil person as the newspaper had portrayed him. "He was caught in the wrong place at the wrong time with the wrong crowd," she concluded.

Heather was struggling with the reality that someone she cared about had done something she knew was wrong. She just couldn't admit that he had a dark side, so what did she do? Like most of us, she blamed his behavior on the bad crowd. Later, when the Smith boys were interviewed, their mother said the same thing. "All three of my sons are good boys. They never meant any harm. They were just influenced by the wrong group."

A bad crowd is any group of persons unwilling to admit they have a bad side. Other people might admit it, but they usually don't. It's easy to recognize the dark, shadowy side of other people, but when it's us and our friends, it's almost impossible to see. We fight to protect our good picture of ourselves and those we care about. We squirm and twist until we can see our behavior in the best possible light. We don't like to see the shadow that follows our close friends and relatives. Although Christians are supposed to see the best in people and we aren't to spread gossip, it doesn't mean we are to overlook the shadowy, dark side—even in our friends. Even our friends have a shadow, a bad side or a dark self. The apostle Paul confessed that he was a sinner—that which he ought to do, he did not at times and vice versa.

If we just excuse the dark side and wrongdoings of our friends, we can't help them in the long run. We and they must accept their dark sides in order for them to find forgiveness and to want to grow. Our refusal to accept the dark sides of friends could confuse them personally and rob them of the opportunity to confess and seek reconciliation. Of course, we know that accepting the shadow side of a friend means accepting our own dark sides. We all have sinned and fallen short of the glory of God. To accept the shadow of a family member or a friend is difficult; however, not to accept it will ultimately be the end of our friendship. There's a dark, ugly, bad side in all of us; our only hope is to recognize it, accept it, and turn toward the light. As long as we refuse to see ourselves as potentially a part of the bad crowd, then we are doomed not to grow. When we can honestly accept our limitations, we can more easily deal with them, accept forgiveness, and continue our spiritual pilgrimage.

Discussion Questions

What do you think is the dark side of most persons?

Can the wrong crowd influence individuals to do something they otherwise would not do?

If the crowd influences an individual, is the individual no longer guilty?

How can we accept the dark sides of our friends and still be their friends?

Have you ever felt rejected because persons saw only your shadow? How did you feel? What do you wish could have been done about it?

Friendships represent a significant element of a teenager's support system. As one listens to youth's stories, understanding their peer relationships opens up new avenues of insight. Another significant window into young persons' lives is their feelings.

7

Feeling Stories

Adolescents' stories are packed with feeling, emotion, and pathos. The world of the teenager is a world of feelings. The physiological changes account for some of the feelings. As their glands "kick into gear," they activate a barrage of chemical reactions that do impact their central nervous systems. Mood swings are normal for teenagers.

The newness of much of life produces its own share of affective responses in teens. Each new experience produces a unique sensation. First time experiences abound for young people, each yielding its own set of emotional reactions. Fast, loud, expressive music appeals to teenagers because it reflects their own internal enthusiasm for passion. Their music, like their lives, is packed with shocks, thrills, and throbbing pulsations waiting to be identified. Feelings are to an adolescent as an unexplored jungle must have seemed to Livingstone. While teens may seem impetuous, impulsive, and nearly hysterical, their franticness more realistically reflects a state of intensified emotions rather than an illness.

Distorted thinking does account, however, for a number of negative impressions on the part of adolescents. Youth seem more susceptible to the cognitive distortions discussed by David Burns in his volume *Feeling Good: The New Mood Therapy.* Adolescents may be prone to engage in overgeneralization, all-or-nothing thinking, disqualifying the positive, jumping to conclusions, magnifying the negative, mislabeling emotions, or overpersonalizing an incident.

Overgeneralizing can be seen in the adolescent who doesn't do well on an exam and then concludes, "I guess I'm just stupid anyway. I'll never amount to much." The negative feelings that result from such distortions can lead to further distortions.

All-or-nothing thinking is reflected in a statement like, "I can't stay on my diet; I just keep eating one piece of candy after another. I've eaten another piece of candy—I may as well 'pig out' on the whole box." Teens are certainly capable of more complex reasoning, but, frequently, they do not use it to analyze their own actions.

Adolescents frequently disqualify the positive with statements like, "Oh, they really don't mean that." Or, "So, I did make one good grade; that doesn't mean I'll make more."

Jumping to conclusions, another typical adolescent distortion, could be seen in statements like, "The teacher didn't call on me today. I guess he knew I wasn't prepared; he's not going to give me that recommendation to go to college after all."

Magnifying the negative—another common error that leads to hurtful, painful, and shameful emotions on the part of teenagers—is reflected in "Did you hear him critique me in band today? I bet I'll be put back into the beginner's band." Or, "I got a B in algebra. I know I'll never make the National Honor Society."

Mislabeling emotions, a frequent point of confusion for teenagers, is readily observable when they discuss love. One teenage girl said to me, "I get so excited when he drives up in that sports car, I just love him so much." A teenage boy remarked that he knew he loved a particular girl because she aroused him sexually. On further reflection, he allowed that actually most any girl caused him to feel that way.

Teenagers personalize situations and often create negative emotions for themselves. Their egocentric behavior leads them naturally to such distortions. For example, one teenage girl reflected, "My parents are fighting over how much to spend for Christmas. I know it's all my fault." Another said, "Our youth minister moved to another church. He must not like me very much. I would have thought he would stay here at least until I graduated from high school."

Usually adolescents need assistance in verbalizing and labeling their feelings. I have found a series of questions helpful in guiding them to gain control of their emotions rather than to remain the victim of their feelings.

Feeling Questions

At the end of a workshop on learning to understand and use emotions constructively, a group of teenagers put together the following feeling statements. When asked to complete the sentence "Sometimes I feel," they offered some of the following responses:

"Sometimes I feel . . .
  . . . free, like a gull gliding in a warm summer's breeze."
  . . . peaceful, like a turtle sunbathing on a half-submerged log."
  . . . excited, like a puppy jumping around in autumn leaves."
  . . . powerful, like an eagle soaring upward on a thermal current."
  . . . loving, like a parent standing over a newborn baby's crib."
  . . . cuddly, like a puppy snuggled in my lap."
  . . . afraid, like a lone quail zigzagging through a barrage of bullets."
  . . . guilty, like a fat fox caught in the henhouse."
  . . . anxious, like a newborn gazelle wobbling on weak, stiltlike legs."
  . . . warm, like a cat daydreaming by the fireplace."
  . . . depressed, like a lonely goose flying homeward in a gray drizzle.
  . . . frustrated, like a tired rat in a never-ending maze."
  . . . angry, like a caged animal longing for the wilderness."
  . . . embarrassed, like a goat in a style show for sheep."
  . . . lonely, like the last person chosen on the team."

Six questions assist teenagers in sorting out the big, buzzing mass of confused feelings associated with their stories. These questions are:
  What is it?
  How strong is it?
  What and who makes it?
  Whose is it?
  So what now?
  What else feels like it?

These simple questions frequently require complex dialogue for satisfactory answers. Adolescents who can answer these six questions will have a grip on their feelings and not be as victimized by impulsive behavior motivated by being out of touch with their feelings. For example, a teenager might say, "I just can't stand my father. He drives me up the wall." While this statement is at one level a description of the tension between the father and the son, it is at a different level a statement of feelings.

So the first question would be, What is it? The teenager might say, "I don't know. I can't give it a name. I just feel like running away, I feel like screaming, or I feel like telling him to go jump in the lake." Often, I will use a multiple-choice question with teens to help them answer the what-is-it, how-do-you-name-your-feeling, question. I simply ask, "Are you mad, sad, bad, or glad?" These general direction words help them locate the feeling. Most likely the above-mentioned teenager would say, "Well, I guess I'm mad. But I kind of feel bad because you're not supposed to be mad at your father." *Mad* and *bad,* while general words, do help to focus the feeling somewhat.

To answer the what-is-it question further, I draw a continuum—zero to one hundred—and call it the mad feeling. I ask the teenager to help me locate some words on that continuum that might be synonyms for *mad,* such as is done in the illustration below.

Assisting teenagers to name the feeling in this manner also begins to answer the how-strong-is-it question. If the feeling is generally *mad,* and they locate it around the 75 percent level and agree that they might use the word or any synonym for that point, then we and the adolescents understand their feelings as very intense.

What and who makes it that way are questions that focus on activity and personhood. The teenager has answered who makes it that way by saying that his father makes him angry or so frustrated or so upset or whatever word he would choose. What makes one angry focuses on specific behavior. Thus the story might unfold with the question, "Tell me some specific things your father does that irritate you so intensely?" The youth might say that his father drinks or pushes him—or it may be something mild like switching the TV channels. In the conversation, it would be up to the caregiver and the teenager to assess if the anger is proportionate to the cause. If the father switches

TV channels and that's all, 75 percent on the anger scale seems rather intense. Perhaps the youth is overreacting. If the father stomped and smashed a radio that the teenager had purchased with his own money because he had refused to turn it down or didn't hear his father, then the teenager might be justified in such an intense reaction.

The fourth question "Whose is it?" focuses on the responsibility of the teenagers to claim their own feelings. Granted, feelings are generated by the actions of those around us; thus, we ask, What makes you feel this way? But, ultimately, we can choose our responses to a given context. I become angry when people abuse me. I become excited at ball games. I feel guilty when I don't live up to my own expectations. I become sad when I lose a good friend. Learning to put *I* in front of a feeling word can become an important step in writing one's own feeling stories with accuracy and power.

Occasionally, teenagers do not want to accept responsibility for working out their feelings. "So what now?" focuses their attention on the need to act responsibly through the feelings. They can rewrite the rest of the story between themselves and those around them, particularly their families. "So what now?" is a way of asking, What are your alternatives in dealing with the situation that leaves you feeling this way? Basically, they have three alternatives: change something, tolerate it, or leave. Adolescents need to look realistically at their capacities to change and tolerate. Particularly in relationships with their family, leaving would be a last resort. However, in extreme cases such as abuse, they may need to choose the leave alternative.

"What else feels like that?" is a question that helps teenagers associate feelings with other experiences. They might say, "This feels like I felt when my coach kicked me off the team," or, "I feel like I felt when I didn't do my homework and the teacher gave me detention after school." Learning to associate groups of feelings also facilitates focusing the feeling on the appropriate response. For example, a teen might be angry with a parent but taking it out on a peer or vice versa.

As we assist teenagers in telling their stories, guiding them to understand, discuss, and be responsible for their feelings adds a significant dimension to the story. Feelings are to the descriptions of the behavior what music is to a television drama. The facts of the story are what we see and the dialogue we hear. The music sets the feeling tone. Light, airy woodwind music usually notes joy, safety, and happiness. Low, bass, dissonant music often denotes anger or danger. Adding the feeling assists teens in completing their story and in understanding the complete story. Feelings help them express the inexpressible.

Often, a story captures feelings in ways that the questions fail to capture. For example, a teenaged girl whose boyfriend had been killed in a car wreck experienced intense grief, but she was unable to discuss it with her family and friends. When the question approach to her feelings failed, she did respond to the invitation to tell her favorite story. She selected a story that had become almost a model of life for her. The story was the "Monkey's Paw." You may recall that a magical monkey's paw could grant three wishes. Its owner was about to burn it when a family convinced the owner to let them have it, and they had their three wishes. As their wishes turned sour on them, they developed a kind of hopelessness themselves and ultimately burned the monkey's paw. The girl's story clearly expressed anger, hopelessness, and frustration. As we discussed the feelings, she was able to go back and focus them more carefully and thus free herself from their unconscious control.

Caution must be exercised in dealing with adolescents' feelings, for certainly such an endeavor will stir up feelings for those of us attempting to do so. As we model open, honest, direct communication of feelings, we must be careful not to frighten teenagers by being too intense. While some sharing of feelings is appropriate, most will want to tame down direct expression of feelings with adolescents unless you're in a safe, protective environment. If the adult begins to generate feelings that are frightening, such as love for the teenager or an unhealthy wish to protect the teenager or maybe even the desire to adopt the teenager, it is wise to seek consultation from a personal friend or trusted colleague. Dealing with adolescents' feelings produces a lot of feelings. We can't help the teenagers if we lose control of our own feelings. Before feelings get out of control, we need to make a referral for the teenager to seek help elsewhere. If we can't benefit them, we certainly don't want to create additional crises in their lives.

We also exercise caution to assist teenagers to deal with their feelings appropriately. We don't want them to see our encouragement to express their feelings as a license to "emotionally vomit" on other persons. We know that wild, raging, unchanneled floods of feelings are nonproductive at best and at worst, destructive. However, damming up their emotions and repressing their heart's music can be internally destructive. In talking with youth, we need to assist them to cope with life's highs and lows by talking about the emotions associated with the experience. In so doing, we greatly reduce not only the possibility of destructive behavior, but their desire to turn to pot, pills, or alcohol to escape from their frustration.

Adolescents frequently express feelings indirectly through sarcasm, teasing, flirting, and generally goofing off. The following story illustrates how adults can help teenagers to work through such displaced feelings in a productive manner.

A Funny Thing Happened on the Way to Teasing

"That's not funny," snapped Ginger.

"Then why is everybody laughing?" Buzz sounded off.

As the youth group cackled at Buzz's witty retorts, Ginger went to pieces and left the room in tears. She darted into the kitchen where her mother and some adult friends happened to be sharing memories of their most embarrassing moments. Her mother noticed Ginger's tears and asked, "What's wrong, sweetheart? Are you upset?"

"No, . . . I mean yes . . . um, well, sort of," Ginger stumbled. "The kids are laughing at me just because I spilled punch down the front of this new dress. When I told them it wasn't funny, Buzz shot off some wisecracks, and they laughed even harder at me."

Buzz's mother half gasped. "Why I thought Buzz was sweet on you, Ginger. How could he do a thing like that?" Ginger blushed even more. Just then Buzz burst through the door and exclaimed, "C'mon, Ginger. Don't be upset. I was just teasing. Can't you take a little joke? I'm sorry that you're so thin skinned. You have to admit that slopping punch on your dress was a pretty far-out scene."

Ginger said, "If that's an apology, I accept it. But let me tell you something else, I don't think it was very funny for you to pick on me. Funny is when you laugh with somebody, not at somebody."

"Oh?" Buzz replied. "I really didn't mean to laugh at you, but I see what you mean."

"Well, I guess I can see how you all thought it was good-natured teasing, but you were poking fun at me, and that hurt too much," Ginger accused.

"But, it's not as bad as if we had spilled the punch on you deliberately and set you up," Buzz argued.

Ginger replied hastily, "You better never have pulled some trick like that on me! That really is sick! Fun isn't hurting other people."

"Oh, I don't know," mused Buzz. "Some of the guys drove their car through the principal's front yard the other day. That was sure a laugh."

"I don't think it's funny," Ginger argued. "Any time you hurt somebody or you destroy property, that's taking fun too far."

"Speaking of taking fun too far," Buzz said, "what about when you started teasing me the other day, and three other girls jumped in? I think that was taking it too far."

"Well, maybe," said Ginger. "I didn't invite them to pick on you."

"You didn't stand up for me either," Buzz reminded her.

"I guess it would have been OK," Ginger continued, "since we teased you if I had started laughing at myself about spilling that punch on my dress, then I wouldn't have minded if you had joined in too. It's just that it seems like you were carrying it too far."

"See, like the Bible says," Buzz pontificated, "there's a time to laugh, and a time to cry. I guess knowing when isn't all that easy."

"Oh, it would be if you would stop and think about it," Ginger replied, with a bit of a bite in her tone.

"Funny isn't something I stop and think about," Buzz complained. "When something happens that nobody expects, and you feel like laughing, it's just kind of funny. The situation is there—like when a clown throws a bucket of fake water into a crowd at the circus. Or like when your mom finds a toy spider in your jeans pocket, even when you didn't plant it there. Or like when a puppy trips over its own long ears—that's funny."

"I agree," Ginger said half to herself. "I guess when something's surprising it is usually humorous, but those same things might not be funny if they were tricks on somebody and if somebody were hurt. It's especially not funny then. That's sick humor."

"Yes," Buzz agreed, "but you were not hurt at all when you spilled that punch on your dress."

"Yes, but my feelings were hurt when you laughed at me," Ginger cautiously replied. "I might have laughed, too," Ginger continued, "had it been somebody else."

"See!" Buzz exclaimed. "I wasn't all wrong."

"OK, we're even," Ginger giggled as she pretended to pour her empty punch cup over his head and only a drop fell out.

Questions

Reflect for a moment now on these questions: Do you agree with Buzz's statements or with Ginger's assertions? Why? Was spilling the punch really funny? Was Ginger being too sensitive? What would you have done if you had publicly spilled something on your clothes? Would you even compliment Buzz for creatively teasing you? Could you have laughed with him even if he did laugh first? If you had been Ginger, would you have accepted Buzz's apology? If you had been Buzz, would you have apologized? What do you think Ginger meant when she said she got her feelings hurt?

What makes you laugh? Are you fair to others when you laugh? Discuss with some friends at church or school what they think is funny. Do you agree or disagree? Now, for a real laugh, play the "Funny Game" with your family or friends.

To play the "Funny Game," ask friends to share one humorous thing that has happened that day or to share one of the funniest things that has ever happened to them. Listen for the feelings, not only in the stories but also in the sharing of the stories.

A common phenomenon with teenage stories is a reaction formation. A teenage boy, who for example feels attracted to a girl, might tease her rather than express his attraction directly. She might interpret his behavior as angry, rejecting, or even hostile. Frequently, the feeling line of the teenager's story will be just the opposite of what the behavior might indicate. Sometimes in talking with teenagers, a major breakthrough comes by assigning the opposite feeling to their stories

The following, shared by a junior high girl, illustrates this well.

A Love Story?

"I rushed back to my locker, all out of breath, balancing a stack of books with one hand, trying to hold a candy bar and open my locker with the other. I had trouble remembering the second number although this was the third week of school. Just as the locker was opening, these three boys appeared from nowhere and began to hassle me."

"What's the matter, Sherry? Can't you work those complicated machines?" one of them sneered, as he pointed to a row of lockers.

"Sure, she can," smirked a second boy. "Girls are smarter than boys, aren't they, Sherry?"

"Let me help you," offered a third, as he tipped over my books, only half pretending it was an accident.

"Oh, you leave me alone," I griped. "Go pick on someone else."

"OK, OK, we're leaving," called the leader of the pack. As they wandered down the hallway, I was embarrassed to tears. "I wonder what got into her today?" I heard one of them ask as they walked off.

"I don't know. But, man, isn't she cute?" the other one said.

"I don't understand what they were doing," Sherry puzzled. "I'm confused by all of that. I feel hurt. They were picking on me, then they said I'm cute, and they didn't know what was wrong with me? What in the world makes them act like that?" she wondered.

A few days later, these same young guys were settled into a booth, killing a pitcher of soda pop and declaring war on an extra-large, everything pizza. I asked if I could talk with them for a minute, and they said, "Sure. Want some pizza?"

"No," I replied, patting the overhang at my belt. I asked, "Do you guys know a girl named Sherry?" They turned on like neon signs at the mention of her name. "Wow," one of them said. "Is she one chick!" "Awesome," one replied. "Powerful, really cute," the third one said. I chuckled and said, "You must really think she's special."

"Yeah, but she's kind of weird," the leader commented. "You wouldn't believe what happened the other day." He retold the same story she had told. Here's how they saw it coming down.

"We were walking toward the lunchroom at school, and there she was, struggling to get her locker opened. I wanted to tell her how good she looked. But she probably would have laughed at me. So I said something funny about lockers being complicated machines or something, and she didn't laugh. These two," pointing across the table to his buddies, "started flirting with her. Boy, she really got bent out of shape. So we split the scene. She is kind of strange, I guess."

Questions

Reflect on these questions yourself and perhaps with the teenagers in your life: Were these boys just innocently flirting with Sherry, or did they go too far? Did Sherry get upset too soon? How could she have handled the incident differently? Could she have teasingly said, "Would one of you strong men help me fight off this monster called a locker?" Or, could she have straightforwardly asked, "What are you guys trying to get at anyway?"

Could these guys have avoided the whole embarrassing incident had they been open with their feelings and given her a compliment? If they were flirting, did she have the same right to flirt back?

What feelings did Sherry have? What about the boys? If they had been older, would they have handled the situation any better? How?

Now take a moment and decide who in your life might be sending you one message and meaning another. How can you check out what they really mean? Can you let them know your real feelings?

Remember, teenagers often express feelings they cannot show directly through stories. As we assist them to understand their feelings, we can help them give names, directions, and intensity to their feelings. When we help teenagers identify and own their feelings, we guide them to gain control over their lives. Discussing their feelings is often easier if we can be open and model some of our own feelings—perhaps in story form or perhaps more directly. Finding feelings in the midst of their stories is not difficult. However, it is nearly impossible to sort out fact and fiction in the stories of adolescents. This next chapter will turn our attention to fact-finding stories.

8

Fact-Finding Stories

The first few paragraphs of a well-written report will provide all of the information necessary to understand a given event. Who, what, when, where, how, and why are supplied directly, clearly, and as accurately as possible—not so in the case of most teenage crises stories. As youth retell crises events, adults often complain that they get neither a clear nor detailed picture of what happened. There's an art to helping teenagers be more truthful, specific, and direct in sharing their stories. Many parents have gone out on a limb to protect their own teenagers only to discover embarrassingly, at a later point, that they only had a part of the story. Fact-finding stories are stories adults retell to the teenager, summarizing the teenager's story and intentionally expressing their own bewilderment in why the events do not fit together. This deliberate astonishment presumes the innocence of the teenager but expresses reservations about not being able to fit the story together. One must be careful to avoid accusing the youth and jumping to conclusions as they restate the events in an innocent, questioning way.

For example, when Sean's father asked if I would counsel with Sean and perhaps appear with him in juvenile court at a hearing, I was obviously anxious to get the facts as clearly as possible as I listened to Sean. Sean's initial story went something like this:

> My best friend, Eric, and I were cruising the strip after a movie on Saturday. We met these two guys that Eric knew from another town in the parking lot at the edge of town. We just talked and listened to tapes for a few minutes, and they asked if we could give them a ride back to the restaurant. They said they wanted to meet these girls who had been avoiding their car all night. So we said, sure jump in. One was in the

front seat between Eric and me, and the other stretched out in the back.

We hadn't gone far when the cops met us, turned around, and started following us. "Oh, _____ (expletive deleted)," yelled the one in the back seat. "You'd better step on it! They're after us."

"Man, they're not after us," I protested. Before I knew what happened, the dude in the front seat put his foot over and stepped on the gas. I ran through a stop sign; the cops turned on their blue lights and pulled us over. Before the cop could get to the door, those two guys had split and run down an alley. When the cop asked me to roll down the window, I did. He shined his light in the back seat, and there was a cellophane package of pot laying there. "You'd better get out," he said.

I don't know what happened; I just panicked, gunned it, and tried to drive off. Then, before I'd gone a couple of blocks, there were four police cars after me. They blocked me off at the next alley. Then this cop came up with his gun out, jerked me out of the car, threw me up against the hood, handcuffed Eric, and dragged us off to the station. They're charging me with assault on a police officer."

While there were several elements of Sean's story that seemed plausible, it didn't quite all fit together. I began to retell it, simply: "You mean to tell me, they pulled you over for no reason, and then when you tried to leave, they charged you with assault and battery?" He retold the story slightly differently.

When the "new guy" had put his foot on the accelerator, they reached sixty miles per hour in a thirty-five-mile-per-hour zone. They had rolled the window up on the policeman's arm, were actually dragging him a few feet in the attempt to escape, and they had driven a mile and a half before stopping the second time. The two new guys were wanted in the first place and had used Sean and Eric. The new guys were picked up by the police later. It's not that individuals deliberately misrepresent the truth, although sometimes malicious falsehoods are involved. More often, teenagers blindly see only their side of the incident. Retelling the story helps us get at some of the facts.

A few other questions can further clarify the story. For example, you might ask Sean, "If the police were telling this story, how would they tell it differently? How would each person in the car tell the story? What could you add if you were telling this story to your best friend? Can you think of anything you might have forgotten?"

After gathering data, we are still faced with the process of interpreting the data. We must be careful not to be cast in the role of judge and jury, and we need to refer teenagers and their families for appropriate legal advice when necessary. Nevertheless, even if there are no legal questions to be interpreted, ethical, religious, and interpersonal issues need to be faced. The impact of a given story on an adolescent's image in the community, relationships at school, and perhaps relationships at work all need to be assessed in light of the narrative.

Not only will adolescents and their families need referral to legal resources, they may need help in finding appropriate medical resources. Wise caregivers have a variety of individual and agency phone numbers at their fingertips in order to provide them to the teenagers. Serious caregivers know they cannot provide all that a youth needs. Know when and how and where to make a referral. See Howard Clinebell's *Basic Types of Pastoral Counseling*, revised edition, chapter 12, for pragmatic information on the referral process.

Typically, youth tend to minimize their interpretation of physical danger in personal reporting. They adopt a it-won't-happen-to-me attitude toward danger as their self-defense. A few teenagers have little regard for their own value, show little or no fear of death, and at times will even find excitement in daredevil activities. When such teenagers are depressed, their flippant attitude toward death is a type of passive suicide. For example, a number of teenage boys who enjoy rock climbing frequently take off their safety ropes to tempt death itself. It is not unheard of for such behavior to be a part of driving an automobile, operating dangerous equipment, or jumping from high heights into water. Their interpretation of the facts around the risks easily becomes distorted through their depression and their lack of experience. Frequently, only a severe accident will change the minds of such a group of teenagers. Occasionally, they can be impacted by a television or newspaper account of a crisis in a similar situation.

Requesting teenagers to list on a piece of paper a variety of interpretations to a given event can help them clarify their stories. For example, when Sean was asked to list interpretations for his fleeing from the police, he wrote down the possibility that the two boys they had picked up were wanted by the police, but he also wrote that the police might be looking for a car that just looked like his and pulled him over without a case. When he was asked to list a variety of interpretations to the boys' running from his car and leaving a bag of marijuana in the backseat, his responses varied from he was being used and dumped on to "I guess they could have just forgotten their marijuana."

Levels of Facts

A process of sorting out the levels of communication helps adults and youth understand the mass of confusing data that can arise around a crisis. Four questions have assisted in guiding the process of understanding the levels of communication. They are: What did you observe? What do you think? What do you feel? What did you do? The order of the questions is important in order to avoid distortions based on emotionally filtered data. Two major approaches to understanding personality theory deal with thoughts and feelings in reverse order.

Those of us hoping to help teenagers to tell a story of crisis need to be able to do both. One approach based on psychoanalytic theory is to assist teenagers to ventilate and express their feelings. Feelings are seen as a significant part of reality, and repressed feelings motivate behavior beyond the youths' capacity to control themselves. Repressed feelings are seen as the primary factor in impulsive behavior.

The other school, as represented by behavior/cognitive therapy, proposes that thoughts create emotion. The goal is to help youth avoid painful feelings based on mental distortions. Since feelings are caused by thoughts, thoughts need to be the focus of our conversation. If teenagers learn to perceive more realistically, an enhanced emotional life follows automatically. The thought/feeling controversy will undoubtedly rage on among counselors. Our goal is to assist teenagers to deal appropriately with both. In either case, we must begin with the question, What was observed? What did you see? Hear? Smell? Touch? What was the exact sequence of events? How can that be corroborated? What did it look like from their viewpoint? All of these questions assist in approximating the basic event.

What did you think was going on is the second question. This provides the adolescent's interpretation to the sequence of events. When adolescents can understand that what they think is an interpretation of what they see, then perhaps they will be open to other interpretations of the same event. For example, I often draw the following diagram and ask teenagers what it is.

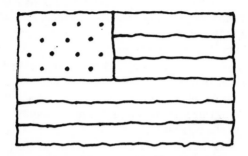

Most often, they will say a flag. I ask them to be more specific, and they will say an American flag. "Well, it could be," I reply. "But how many stripes are on the American flag?" "Thirteen," they respond. "How many stars?" "Fifty," they acknowledge with a smile, realizing that the figure is only a crude approximation of a flag, and they have filled in many missing details in order to think, *It's a flag.* I say, "Well, you're wrong. What you see is a plot of how I'm going to plant my garden. What you called stripes are rows of beans, and what you called stars is where I'm going to sow lettuce." We both observed the same figure, but what we think we see is entirely different. It is based on our associations with the data. What we think is a result of the interaction between our associations and what we actually observed.

Likewise, what we feel is based on the interaction between what we think we have observed and our past associations. If both of us do observe an authentic American flag, our associations with the flag will affect the way we feel. For example, one teenager who participated in his high school ROTC program said he felt an overwhelming sense of pride and joy when he saw the American flag. A second teenager, whose veteran father had died recently, had last seen an American flag at his father's casket. He reported that he felt intense sadness and grief each time he saw an American flag. It is our best associations as well as what we think we are observing that generates our feelings.

This simple illustration may demonstrate how teenagers would feel differently about the same event.

However, sorting out the past associations can be a difficult process in storytelling. Teenagers usually cannot readily identify these past associations and need someone to walk with them through the stories of their past as they begin to identify the ingredients that create their current feelings. For example, a seventeen-year-old girl who had refused for two years to speak to her father was able, after some time, to identify that her major concern was not so much her father but his new wife. After many hours of listening to her stories, it became evident that two or three themes generated her feelings toward the new wife. Partially she blamed the new wife for her parents divorcing in the first place—although the father and mother felt there was no data for such an interpretation. Second, she felt that the new wife had replaced her as "the apple of her daddy's eye." Third, she thought that the new wife was trying to boss her like a mother and had no right to do so. And, finally, she thought that the new wife was too young for her father in the first place. Her interpretations were so strong that for a long period of time she could hear no other story and reach no other conclusions about her parents' divorce and her father's remarriage. After several hours of sharing openly with her father, she was able to sort out some of the interpretations, and they agreed to disagree on others. More importantly, she and her father were able to begin the process of reconciliation and repairing their relationship.

Finally, asking, "What do you intend to do?" or, "What actions need to be taken as a result of this?" can help adolescents accept responsibility for their thoughts and feelings and let go of seeing themselves as helpless pawns in the game of life. Youth regularly tell stories of feeling duped, trapped, and victimized by their parents' decisions. Often, teenagers' blind, impulsive overreactions add to the family crisis. Leading youth to walk carefully through the facts of the crisis can empower them to turn from the danger of the crisis toward the possibilities for growth, reconciliation, and maturity. Remember, God works toward the good in all things. Helping teenagers move through truth toward wholeness reflects hope fitting to the Christian faith.

Ultimately, teenagers must decide how they will act in response to their new interpretations and perhaps clarified feelings about a given event. As storytellers, we may help them by asking one further question: If you could write the best possible ending to this crisis, how would you write it? Asking for the best case scenario creates an image toward which adolescents and their families can work. Of course, not all stories will have a happy ending, but a visualized positive outcome often serves as a lure to pull youth toward personal and family health.

Spying on Yourself

Thus far we have emphasized retelling the story to push the teenager to share all of the details and facts of the story. We have stressed looking at interpretations and helping teenagers and their families be responsible for their interpretation and feelings related to the facts. Often, teens are poor observers of their environment, circumstances, and situation. They need assistance in accurately gathering the facts. Furthermore, like the rest of us, it is difficult to calculate total percentages from casual observation. It is best to write it down.

I often assign teenagers the task of keeping a journal that involves record keeping as homework between our conversations. They are asked to keep a daily record of something like the number of times something good occurs as opposed to the number of times something negative occurs. Remember the young man mentioned earlier who was certain that he had no friends at school. He was assigned to keep a journal, record the number of times each day that he spoke to others at school and the number of times that they pleasantly returned his greetings. To his surprise, over 50 percent of his greetings were returned. This "factual proof" confirmed that his statement "no one likes me at school" was an obvious error. It also assisted him in his self-image, battle against depression, and perceived loneliness.

Homework can be assigned as a research project in which the teens are asked to record a number of activities about themselves. Such record keeping helps them confront generalizations, hasty conclusions, and stereotypical thinking. For example, a young lady was asked to keep a list of daily chores she performed and those performed for her by other family members. She had made the comment that her parents treated her "like a slave" and expected too much from her.

Rather than argue with her statement, assigning the fact-finding mission gave her an opportunity to prove to me or herself the real nature of the circumstance. Granted, even the daily record of her observations were her interpretations of the events, but they, at least, provided a starting place. She returned a week later, laughing at herself.

"Let me see your research journal," I asked.

"You won't believe it; I didn't either," she said. She had recorded the amount of work that her mother had done in cooking and doing her laundry; her father had worked on her headphones, fed her pets, and helped her with homework. She had listed approximately three hours of work she had done during the week. However, compared to the nearly twelve hours her parents had given her, she could not continue to live with her accusation that they were making her a slave. Scrutinizing their activities in a quest for the real facts had given her a new appreciation for her own family. Teaching teenagers to observe accurately, record carefully, and interpret fairly can be an important activity that continues beyond the written homework assignments. Before they can let their "yea be yea, and their nay be nay," they need to know what is yes and what is no. As they ferret out the truth, their stories frequently change.

Getting at the facts, an important process in helping youth in crises, can be a significant part of building a relationship with any teenager. Look at their view of things from a different perspective.

What's in a T-Shirt?

A popular youth minister related a positive experience with T-shirt Sunday. Youth were asked to wear their favorite T-shirts and be prepared to answer the question: "What's in the shirt?" Many youth collect a wide variety of T-shirts as statements of their identity, affirmations of groups to which they belong, or as an expression of their feelings. Identity statements can be seen in T-shirts that advertise a product or an establishment where teens have eaten. The "hard-rock" craze of a number of adolescents has been countered by a group of Christian adolescents who wear T-shirts of the "Solid-Rock" variety.

Adolescents claim their identity with a particular group as they wear shirts with their school mascot, church name, or home state name on them. Such T-shirts cause very little conflict with their parents and are the most acceptable in the eyes of adults.

Teens often express a variety of feelings by their choice of T-shirts. On a recent visit to a shopping mall I observed a group of tough guys wearing black shirts with science-fiction-type monsters and angry, threatening slogans across the back. Two girls were wearing identical shirts that somewhat expressed their feeling. The shirts showed a fire hydrant with a dog standing beside it looking expectantly. T-shirts with messages like "Do your own thing," "Just do it," and "Let it happen" also express a variety of feelings.

Persons' feelings are often expressed in their choice of clothing; such was the case with an eighteen-year-old former high school homecoming queen who had been very active in her church. She had some rather serious emotional difficulties after graduation and found herself a patient in the local mental hospital. I had visited her daily and saw only limited improvement. One day when I visited, she shocked me by wearing a T-shirt that said, "You don't have to be crazy to live here, but it helps." At first, I didn't know what to make of her shirt and wasn't sure I should mention it. She brought it up by laughingly saying, "I thought this was really neat for someone who lives in a mental hospital. I won't be here forever, but I think I'm going to keep this shirt around." Her depressed mood was beginning to lift, and she chose the T-shirt as a way of announcing her hope. Her ability to laugh at herself also indicated a sign of improvement.

Not all youth are aware of why they choose the T-shirts or other clothing that they select. However, assisting them in observing the shirt, thinking about it, and expressing associated feelings can help them understand the stories they tell through the costumes they wear.

Parent/youth conflicts erupt regularly around clothing. Youth can use their choice of clothing to express independence or rebellion, or even an all-out power struggle between them and their parents. The above-mentioned process of helping youth understand how their attire serves as a signboard to the world can also be used to facilitate parents' understanding of their teenagers' wardrobes. Parents may over- or misinterpret what is meant by a given T-shirt. "Clothes make the man," argued one father, as he tried to convince his eighteen-year-old son not to wear a shirt advertising a particular rock group. "That group certainly does not stand for Christian values," continued the father. "I know it doesn't," said the boy, "but I don't think wearing this shirt means I have to agree with everything they say. A lot of criminals wear three-piece suits, but that doesn't mean when our pastor wears one that he agrees with them, does it?" the boy retorted.

Parents who can learn to make matter-of-fact statements about what they observe in their youths' outfits, what they think it means, how they feel about it, and who then ask the youth how they respond to it, can initiate profitable dialogue between themselves and their teenagers. Parents who overreact to an adolescent's garb are likely to push the youth further away. Occasionally, parents can even identify with the youth and wear similar clothing themselves. A low-key, non-defensive discussion about clothing and what it means usually produces the best results, for parents and youth.

When parents and youth are conflicting around clothes, youth will frequently argue with something like, "You can't judge a book by its cover." To an extent that is true. Certainly one does not know everything about a teenager simply from the choice of the teenager's clothing. Just as one must thoroughly engage a book in order to understand it, time, energy, and understanding are needed to fully understand a teenager. But on the other hand, the book didn't pick its cover, and someone did attempt to communicate something about the book by its cover design. Likewise, adolescents who do choose to put on their own "covers" need to be aware that it communicates to other persons. Accepting responsibility for the results of one's choices is a significant part of the maturing process. Teenagers who can live with the fact that their clothes do make a statement will find life less confusing and perhaps even less disappointing.

One young man complained repeatedly that although he was bright, talented, and industrious, he could not get a job. After several minutes of dialogue, I thought to ask how he dressed for his job interviews. "Like this," he replied, pointing to his jeans with a hole in the knee and his T-shirt. "This is who I am. If they don't want me for who I am, they don't want me." His T-shirt, which had a saxophone and cymbals on it, read at the bottom, "Sax Cymbal." While it was certainly cute and perhaps humorous, it was by no means impressive nor indicative of his own statements of the kind of worker he would be. Accepting responsibility for verbal communication is difficult enough. Attempting to assist adolescents to own up to the power of their nonverbal statements through their clothing can be an uphill battle. The following week when I met with the teenager, I, too, dressed down, wearing a pair of jeans, tennis shoes, and a fishing shirt. His first comment was: "What gives with you, dude? I've never seen you look like this around the church."

"What difference does it make?" I asked. "I was just working in my garden and decided to come on over." Before I continued he got the point.

"Pretty sneaky, pretty sneaky," he said. "I walked right into your trap, didn't I? I reacted to your clothing although you're still the same person I talked with last week."

"You are insightful," I said to him. That day we talked about his relationship with his parents and said very little about job interviews.

Three days later he called to inform me that he had a job as an errand boy in an office downtown. "By the way," he concluded the conversation, "I have to wear a dress shirt and a tie. Can you believe it?" he laughingly closed off.

Clarifying the facts in adolescents' stories moves us in the direction of dealing with truth, reality, and the essence of the teenagers' world. Nevertheless, we must be cautious and realize the inexactness of all conversation. Attacking a teenager's story in the pursuit of objective, scientific-type data can widen the generation gap between adults and youth. Some aspects of the stories are best left symbolic. Since ultimate reality lies beyond total understanding, learning to live with images of the truth strengthens our bond with teens. As we seek reality together, we and the teens must admit that now we see through a glass dimly; only in eternity can we expect to see all of truth face-to-face.

The ultimate story is the story of faith. Before we share faith stories from the past and our own faith stories, we are wise to listen to the faith stories of today's youth.

9

Faith Stories

Faith means many things. Faith can refer to belief in God or to the fidelity and loyalty of one's promises. Generally, one's faith refers to one's system of religious beliefs. James Fowler, in *Stages of Faith,* refers to faith as the process, not the content, of one's beliefs. It is understanding how the Ultimate orders one's life in relationship to self and others. Ask a group of streetwise teenagers to define faith, and most will say, "Religion." Ask a group of churchwise adolescents, and many will quote Hebrews 11:1: "Faith is the assurance of things hoped for, the conviction of things not seen." Ask both groups what they mean and be prepared for stumbling silence.

Adolescents paint pictures, tell stories, sing songs, and construct symbols to point to their faith, but they seldom directly address the content of their faith. This concluding chapter will rest upon a general definition of faith as one's belief about God and how that affects seeing ourselves and our relationship to others.

The Faith Stance of Teenagers

Numerous studies have measured the rise and fall of teenagers' participation in organized religion. This may or may not tell us much about their spiritual conditions and faith stance. Depending on an adolescent's attitude toward faith, faith stories will be used for various purposes.

An Unawareness of Faith

A number of adolescents grow up unaware of faith issues. They receive no formal religious training. Public displays of religions are perhaps discounted by their parents and other authority persons. Religious holidays are times for family picnics and vacations. Religious observances on radio and television are the object of ridicule, scoffing, and mockery. Thoroughly secular young people abound in contemporary society. Such teens are uninformed concerning organized religion, but more importantly, they are unaware and out of touch with transcendent elements of themselves. While a few such adolescents have reached their positions through deliberate teachings from their parents, most are in this unaware state through neglect.

For those unaware of religious experience, faith stories awaken them to the dimensions of the Ultimate. Stories sensitize them to the realm of religious reality. Faith stories stimulate and provoke a fascination, interest, and desire to know and experience the eternal Supreme Being. A number of teenagers, deprived of faith stories, have been lured by stories of the demonic and the powers of Satan. When followers of the Creator of heaven and earth failed to inform them, their hunger opened them to hear the stories of the underworld.

A Rejection of Faith

A second category of the faith stance of adolescents, rejection, also challenges the church for a response. No small number of teenagers oppose the faith of their childhood and express disgust toward the church. Daniel Aleshire, professor of psychology and Christian education, notes that youth do not readily separate the content of their beliefs from either the people who believe it or the institutions that believing people create. He goes on to add that youth reject their faith because of relationships with an unhealthy church, sinful people, or disappointing experiences (Aleshire, 112).

The faith stories that can reconnect such youth with their religious pilgrimage will most likely need to be presented in subtle, delicate, and wise formats so as not to be rejected without a hearing. Symbolic stories with a penetrating message may need to be presented in a secular format, such as retelling the story of the prodigal son in a contemporary setting. Occasionally, stories from history, Greek mythology, or other cultures can be used to begin the process of religious dialogue. Adolescents who have rebelled against their family's faith, perhaps even renounced all religious commitment, have so hardened their hearts as to need to hear the gospel in a fresh light.

A Borrowed Faith

A third faith stance of some adolescents is borrowed faith. A number of seemingly religious teenagers have not been on a spiritual journey but rather have learned to pay lip service to their parents' beliefs. However, these beliefs have little or no impact on their personal lifestyles, commitments, and values. Such was the case with the former homecoming queen who was active in church but still depressed enough to be hospitalized (see ch. 8). There comes a time when the young person must voluntarily make a decision concerning the Christian faith. As the individual matures, a personal affirmation can take many forms. Aleshire points out that while some find real affirmation "quietly, peaceably and almost imperceptibly, for others it comes only after battles, denials, and wrestling."

Storytelling with adolescents whose faith has been borrowed from their parents needs to awaken them to this personal dimension. Stories that confront, challenge, and charge them with the responsibility to own their religious experience can nurture them in the faith. The story of Esther and her struggle to be faithful to God's call might be an excellent story with which to begin the process of challenging young adults to examine their own relationship to God and their willingness to sacrifice as a result of that relationship.

A Seeking Faith

A fourth faith stance, seeking faith, includes a large number of youth who are committed to their Christian experience but are dissatisfied with their own lack of spiritual maturity. These teenagers sincerely seek after maturity in faith. They want discipleship experiences that lead them beyond talking about religious experience into experiencing authentic encounters with the Ultimate. They are striving for a faith to take into the marketplace of their lives. They sincerely desire to walk with God and to know God's will for their lives, but they lack experiences that have matured them in the faith.

For these adolescent seekers, stories that inform them of the content of the Scripture and expose them to the challenges and decisions of everyday life can foster their spiritual maturity. Stories that present ethical alternatives in the context of the teenage world benefit seekers perhaps more than any other faith-stance group. Stories like the son who felt under rewarded for finding his father's lost dog, the unforgiving servant, or the story of Janice who slept with another man out of anger with her boyfriend (see ch. 3) work well with teens seeking a mature faith.

A Pilgrim Faith

Another category is pilgrim. There are spiritually maturing adolescents who see their Christian experiences as a pilgrimage and a journey toward spiritual wholeness. They know God as a personal Companion, have a sense of having God at the center of their very being, and permit this center to inform their decision making as well as relationships to others. Families, friends, and extended community recognize in them this spiritual maturity.

Youth who are on a spiritual journey need stories that sustain them in the process. Such stories can be of a devotional nature, but they are particularly helped by biographical accounts of spiritually mature persons. Adolescents on a spiritual pilgrimage can profit greatly from writing down their own religious experience and sharing the journals with other such adolescents or with a spiritual guide or mentor. An eighteen-year-old, maturing youth shared that Wayne E. Oates's autobiography, *The Struggle to Be Free,* served as hope and inspiration to struggle with faith issues.

Knowing a youth's faith stance is important before we approach them with a faith story. However, their faith stories can be used quite effectively in understanding their need for further spiritual growth. I have found it effective to ask them to share their favorite Bible stories.

Using Favorite Bible Stories

A number of questions can be used to help teenagers understand their perception of God, relationships to others, and sense of self from a clearer perspective. I usually ask teenagers for their favorite Bible stories; perhaps they will choose to share just a verse or favorite Bible character. Alongside those questions, I will ask them to describe significant religious experiences and, particularly, to discuss their beliefs and practices about prayer and Bible study. For example, in a recent discussion, a bright, older adolescent picked Moses as her favorite Bible character and the story of Moses confronting Pharaoh with the plagues as her favorite Bible story. As she described her own religious experience, it became clear that she had a real sense of herself as a leader of God's people. However, she also shared that she didn't feel very close to God, and she was angry at her church. She had longed for the power to bring down the plagues on her spiritual enemies. She had long since reduced prayer to the level of before-meal rituals and had all but ceased serious Bible study. There are a number of categories that I found helpful in examining the stories adolescents share to understand their relationship with God, others, and themselves.

Polarities That Can Facilitate Understanding of God

Since adolescents can cognitively deal effectively with paradox and ambiguity, I suggest to them a series of polarities that might facilitate their understanding of God. Seven polarities that I have found particularly helpful may be revealed through the stories they select, but likely these will need follow-up conversation for further exploration of how they see God.

Trust versus suspicion.—The first polarity concerning an adolescent's understanding of God is trust versus suspicion. Does the adolescent have a basic sense of trust toward God and religious institutions? Does the adolescent balance that with a healthy suspicion that "test the spirits" in relationship to knowing God, particularly through religious institutions? A balance between trust and suspicion facilitates faith growth. Teens who are overly suspicious or so trusting as to be gullible may have some difficulty. One boy was so suspicious of God that he feared talking to a "real minister." A naive fifteen-year-old got pregnant—she believed that God would keep her from conceiving if she just prayed before having sex with her boyfriend.

Faith versus doubt.—A second polarity concerning an adolescent's attitude toward God and experiences with God, faith versus doubt, is similar to trust versus suspicion and yet different. Trust is based more on the observable and faith on the unobservable, as used here. Adolescents who have a healthy sense of trust in God, and in religious institutions, will be able to express their doubts about their understanding of God. Those who have excessive doubt and those whose faith cannot be put to the test, so to speak, are not as likely to mature and grow spiritually.

Saul of Tarsus exemplified excessive suspicion as he persecuted the followers of Christ. Nevertheless, in his trust of God through his own conversion experience on the road to Damascus, Paul's faith developed to the point that he could share his former struggle with a lack of faith openly with others. Paul could confess that he was a pilgrim without destroying his faith.

Law versus grace.—A third polarity useful in assessing an adolescent's understanding of God is law versus grace. Again, neither can be cast aside, but both must be held in a state of healthy tension for the sake of spiritual maturity. Jesus did not come to replace the law but to fulfill the law. Teenagers who attempt to throw aside the law of God and live without limits obviously will not grow spiritually. However, youth who cast away God's grace live in spiritual bondage to the law and miss the forgiving nature of God. This healthy balance between law and grace is an important dimension of God's nature for adolescents to understand. On the one hand, they know the firm requirements of faith, and on the other, they can accept forgiveness as God's gift of grace to sinful humanity.

God's power as over against God's supposed weakness.—This fourth polarity to be dug out from the stories adolescents tell about God, particularly from their favorite Bible passages, deals with God's power. In a recent Sunday School class, a teenager was struggling with God's involvement in the automobile-related death of one of her friends. On the one hand, the power of God seemed absolute to her, but on the other, she had prayed that her Christian friend would not die. And when the friend died, she questioned the power of God and began to look at God as weak. After some in-depth Bible study, she was able to affirm that God allowed certain things to happen in order to preserve the freedom God had given all persons. She could see God's permissive will as somewhat weaker than her earlier view of

God who controlled all things at all times in all ways. Living in the tension between God's authority and God's permissive will was an ambiguity she could accept.

God's love versus God's wrath.—Another polarity useful in understanding an adolescent's faith experience and pilgrimage is God's love versus His wrath. Some see God as only loving; others see Him only as filled with wrath and disdain for all of creation. For example, the teenager who chose Moses as her favorite Bible character and retold the story of the plagues saw God as angry at all creation and believed that she and others could only earn God's love by being faithful like Moses. It was a difficult struggle for her to believe John 3:16-17: "For God so loved the world that he gave his only Son, that whoever believes in him should not perish but have eternal life. For God sent the Son into the world, not to condemn the world, but that the world might be saved through him." Maintaining love and wrath as opposites broadens teenagers' understanding of God.

Order versus chaos.—A further polarity concerning the nature of God useful in understanding adolescent's faith experience is order versus chaos. Is the universe ordered and within the control of the sustaining Creator, or do we live in a chaotic, random environment out of God's control? Most teenagers prefer to hope for an ordered universe, but they understand the chaotic elements of nature such as hurricanes, earthquakes, and tornados to be a part of creation. Seeing order and chaos as opposed to each other permits teenagers to experience the nature of God as beyond their full knowing, but it sustains them in their quest for answering questions such as, "Why do good things happen to bad people?"

Active versus passive.—A seventh polarity, active versus passive, is often seen in adolescents' choice of faith stories. While most youth see God as active, alive, and involved in the world, a few hold to the view that God is unconcerned, uninvolved, and distant. Those with a more passive view of God seem to have a wintery-type religion that focuses on suffering with feelings of hopelessness. Those who have an exclusively active view of God, however, are likely to see only the good times and have a shallow, summery-type of religion that fails to sustain them in a time of crisis. An appropriate balance is necessary.

Polarities That Can Facilitate Understanding of Others

As adolescents discuss their faith stories, a number of polarities can be used in assessing their relationships with other persons. Family members, church members, and persons in society at large are seen in a particular light through the teenager's faith stance.

Trust versus suspicion.—In listening to adolescents' favorite Bible passages, I listen again for a theme of trust versus suspicion in the nature of their relationship to others. This polarity also seen as central in their relationship to God undergirds all other polarities in their relationship to family, church, and society. Adolescents need a basic trust in order to function with others, and yet a degree of suspicion is necessary to avoid being so naive as to be vulnerable.

The story of the good Samaritan has been useful in examining the trust versus suspicion ends of a continuum. What are the trust and mistrust issues with the robber? with those who passed by? and, of course, with the good Samaritan? One particularly untrusting youth said, "There's no way the Samaritan would have stopped to help. How did the Samaritan know he wasn't faking it and just another robber going to take all that he had?"

Good versus bad.—Another polarity useful in examining adolescents' attitudes toward others is good versus bad. Teens can err by embracing either end of that continuum to the exclusion of the other. Those who see others as totally good are blinded to the sinful nature of humanity and the world. Those who see all of society as bad can become prophets of doom whose faith has little to offer by way of relationships. A favorite poem shared often with adolescents reflects the ambiguous nature of this antithesis:

> There is so much good in the worst of us,
> And so much bad in the best of us,
> That it hardly behooves any of us
> To talk about the rest of us.
>
> —Edward Wallis Hoch

Open versus closed.—A third polarity useful in assessing adolescents' stance toward others is open versus closed. How involved in family and society is the young person, as opposed to how closed off from interactions with others? Teens need a degree of openness in order to grow in their relationships. However, a degree of closedness is necessary to protect their identity from being engulfed by others. While it is true that no teen is an island, it is also true that every teen must have some protection from the oceans of others who would swallow up their identity. Open and closed issues can frequently be seen around the desire to "stay on the mountaintop and build a tabernacle." Some teens want to cut themselves off from society. They would find an ascetic life-style appealing. The young man who refused even to talk with his physician and the psychiatric staff was too closed. When the teenaged girl let a stranger take her home from a party, she was too open.

Giving versus getting.—This fourth polarity in assessing an adolescent's faith stance toward others again requires acceptance of both ends of the continuum. While selfish, hoarding, materialistic adolescents may see others only in terms of what they can get from them, teenagers who become so giving as to be like a doormat also fail in their relationships. Teens who have a healthy sense of the balance between getting and giving in their family, church, and society grow and mature spiritually more than those who are at either end of the continuum. Certainly, the lad who gave his fishes to feed the five thousand must have received enough for a portion of lunch himself. Giving and getting are important dimensions of youth's relationship to others.

Some teenage boys see girls only as people from whom to get sex. While doing premarital counseling with a nineteen-year-old young man and his eighteen-year-old bride-to-be, I requested that they write out "ideal vows." Hers were filled with mutuality and love; his were self-centered and focused on getting. We had much to discuss.

Love versus disdain.—Similar to the love-and-wrath polarity of teens' relationship with God is the fifth polarity: love versus disdain. Youth who have a disdain for others often harbor a large amount of unresolved anger. They enjoy seeing others suffer and have very little love for humanity. Youth who love everybody can be equally at risk because they have no sense of protecting themselves from the sin in the world. First Corinthians 13 can be a helpful passage in assisting adolescents to understand the nature of love. Frequently, I ask them to read this passage and to write a love story that shows how they live it out in their own families. With older adolescents, the story can be refocused to how they would live it out in a dating relationship. Nicki, who got half her hair shaved off, discovered who loved her enough to stay by her and who did not.

Inclusion versus exclusion.—A final dimension of youths' relationships with others, inclusion versus exclusion, assesses the degree to which they feel they belong to the community. Some adolescents feel excluded from their own families, others feel excluded from the community of faith. Inclusion and exclusion are particularly significant issues around adolescents' struggle with stepfamilies, adoption, and sibling rivalry. These issues can also be seen in their relationship to the church. Many teens feel their church looks down on adolescents and has very little place for them. Frequently, youth point to the portion of the church budget spent for youth activities to substantiate their feelings of being excluded from the community of faith. The amount of time adults spend with teenagers and the general interest they show in youth are further indicators of their levels of commitment.

When a family moves to a new community, inclusion becomes a major issue for their teens. Youth need assistance from parents, teachers, and ministers as they break into a new group.

Polarities That Can Facilitate Understanding of Self

Having examined seven polarities that guide our understanding of teenagers' views of God and seven for their views of others, we now turn to a set of issues that focus our attention on their views of the self.

Guilt versus innocence.—The first polarity that is useful in working with teens' view of their self is guilt versus innocence. Occasionally, stories reveal a sense of whether or not the youth see themselves, other persons, and in particular other teenagers as "dirty" or "clean" before God. Adolescents need to maintain the tension between these opposites. Those who have only a "dirty" view of humanity lose sight of the sense of the power of God to mediate forgiveness as a gift of grace. However, those who have an overly optimistic, clean, and innocent view of humanity tend not to take sin seriously. Maintaining an appropriate tension between the two seems to work best for youth.

One girl thought she had committed the unpardonable sin by shoplifting a five-dollar item. While shoplifting is indisputably wrong, it is not unforgivable. Her "dirty" view of humanity isolated her from God's forgiveness. A young man saw nothing wrong with his promiscuous sexual behavior as long as he paid for any abortions. His "clean" view kept him from recognizing the sinfulness of his actions and allowed him to hurt others.

Directed versus aimless.—This second polarity can be seen in the sense of the youths' awareness of the purpose of life from the stories they select. Youth who have an overdeveloped sense of direction in their lives are likely to close their decision-making process early and miss opportunities for development as well-rounded persons. On the other hand, aimless youth who have no goals and for whom the call of God is a foreign term have little sense of motivation. These aimless youth are likely to be caught up by social currents and swept into a life filled only by the quest for more pleasure.

Youth who have a sense of the balance between their direction and aimlessness maintain a flexibility in their sense of direction that leaves them open both to the call of God and to the needs of the world around them. They are more apt to discover meaning and purpose in their adult living.

Bondage versus freedom.—A third polarity to be examined through the faith stories of youth is bondage versus freedom. Bondage, the sense of being a helpless victim under the control of some outside force—be it fate, family, or friends—surfaces regularly as a theme in adolescent storytelling. In fact, it is not uncommon for youth who are on the bondage end of the continuum to say, "I don't know what made me do what I did. I don't understand what came over me." Freedom can be seen in teenagers' stories as they push to determine their own destiny. Youth who totally embrace freedom often fall into the trap of failing to see how their pursuit infringes upon the freedom of others. A balance between bondage and freedom helps teens maintain a sense of responsibility to others as well as responsibility for their own faith pilgrimage. They need to maintain enough sense of freedom to live in hope and enough sense of bondage to live in commitment.

Internal control versus external control.—The fourth polarity that surfaces frequently in adolescent stories deals with internal and external control. James Fowler elevates "locus of control" as one of the major factors in formation of identity. Youth who have a totally internalized locus of control will picture themselves as captains of their own souls and masters of their own fate (Henley, "Invictus"). Such youth who overidentify with internalized locus of control are in danger of undertaking more than they can handle—physically, emotionally, and spiritually. However, youth who err on the external-control side become dependent and look to others for their decision making. Frequently, such youth have grown up in repressive homes and fear the consequences of deciding for themselves. A healthy balance between internal and external control permits adolescents to live in the mutuality of relationships. Their relationship with God, church, and family will be balanced better if they maintain a healthy sense of tension between internal and external control.

Discipline versus capricious behavior.—A fifth polarity that sometimes surfaces in adolescents' faith stories is discipline versus capricious behavior. While few youth err on the side of excessive discipline, those who do could wind up with behavior disorders. Obsessive, compulsive youth are likely to have both a disciplined view of themselves and an internal locus of control. They can become so constricted and restricted in life as to be unable to function. Youth, for example, may become socially withdrawn in an attempt to discipline themselves from temptation. On the other hand, a youth who is extremely disciplined and living with an external sense of control may enslave himself or herself to a cultic guru. Cults exploit genuine, honest youth seeking a sense of external discipline for their lives. In a way, this is an indictment of the church's failure to require enough of young disciples.

The youth who embrace the capricious side of these counterparts are likely to display erratic, impulsive behavior with little awareness of the results of their actions for the lives of others. The consequences of their impulsive behavior concerns them little. Their behavior can become rebellious, antisocial, and potentially harmful to themselves or others. Teenagers who have a balance between discipline and capricious behavior have the capacity to control themselves when necessary without in any way reducing their capacity for joyful celebration. While they remain committed to the teachings of their faith, they are open to new experiences.

Inclusion versus exclusion.—The final theme that surfaces frequently around self-identity in youths' stories is inclusion versus exclusion. Youth have a sense of themselves as belonging to or not belonging to the people of faith. Teens who live only on the inclusion side blindly accept all that is taught them, and they run the danger of letting their religion become little more than a sense of belonging to an organization. However, those who live on the exclusion side see religion and the grace of God available only to other persons. Through experiences like baptism, their first Lord's Supper, youth choir, and discipleship training, youth receive a sense of belonging to their faith group. A balance between inclusion and exclusion enables them to speak to the faith group and to alter its sense of direction. Youth with a healthy sense of balance between inclusion and exclusion are likely to become the leaders of religious institutions in the next generation.

These polarities serve as guidelines in understanding the faith stories of adolescents. They can be applied to the young person's choice of favorite Bible stories or youth stories about faith heroes or even teenagers' stories about their own faith experiences. Maintaining a healthy tension between the polarities creates a balance where the adolescent has a degree of aliveness, flexibility, and openness to the future. Such a stance maximizes opportunities for faith growth.

While adults are certainly important guides for the faith journeys of adolescents, youth can guide each other in significant ways. Teens who share their faith stories with one another and commit themselves through small groups to the processes of discipleship can enrich one another's faith experience.

Faith Stories

Diary excerpts, poems, and stories shared by adolescents provide rich insight into their spiritual awareness. Oftentimes as they grapple to express their hunger, they seem unaware of the thousands of pilgrims who have gone before them. Ultimately, each youth discovers his or her own unique path and writes a new personal story one chapter at a time.

The following poem written by Rodney Culpepper at age thirteen graphically portrays the sense of journey for teenagers. Adolescence is the pilgrimage from childhood to adulthood. While teens may not fully comprehend their struggle, they tell the story of journey as best they can. The understanding of a child will not sustain the journey.

Boating Problems

> I need that boat!
> What boat?
> The boat on the shore!
> What shore?
> The shore you're on!
> That shore?
> No, that boat!
> What boat?
> The wooden boat!
> Wooden?
> Well, maybe it's tin.
> Thin boat?
> No, thick boat, thick boats, thick boots!
> Boots?
> Boots to get to the boat!
> What boat?
> The boat that I need!

The boat poem reflects a sense of struggle between trust and suspicion, faith and doubt, as well as power and weakness and order versus chaos. Adults cannot be certain of the intended audience. This poem reflects a sense of trust versus suspicion toward others, a sense of giving versus getting, as well as a struggle between bondage and freedom. Furthermore, the poem reflects a struggle for direction as over against aimlessness and the theme of internal versus external control. Seeing oneself as committed as over against the apparent fickle nature of the other in the poem indicates a rather strong sense of self-identity for this author.

Another teen poem reflects the groping and seeking nature of adolescence:

> To stare but not see,
> To think but not focus,
> To imagine but not pretend,
> To experience but not understand,
> To daydream . . . such is youth.

Closing Reflections on Guiding New Disciples

The following letter is one example of an approach to use with the youth who is beginning his or her spiritual journey. Each of us encourages teenagers in our own way. This letter is not intended to be inclusive or comprehensive. It merely serves as a beginning point for a discussion around nurturing youth as they write their own record of the gospel story.

A Letter to a New Christian

Dear Maria,

As a young jeanager who has recently made a decision to become a Christian, you will have many persons offering you advice. This letter is for your reflection as you await baptism and wonder what your new experience will bring. Maria, like a newborn baby, a beginning Christian needs a special diet, loving care and a protecting family. Milk, the main diet for an infant, is a complete food. The Scripture likewise is a complete steady diet for Christian strength. Perhaps the Gospel of Mark is a good starting place although Matthew, Luke, and John are preferred by others. Mark is the briefest overview.

When possible, study the Scriptures with others. Regular Bible study guided by those who have prepared themselves will strengthen your faith. In fact, you will grow more quickly if you can memorize a few special passages like John 3:16 or perhaps Psalm 23. You might ask some of your Christian friends what verses they have found to be especially helpful. Infants receive special treatment. They are handled gently, protected from the rough places in life, and provided with plenty of rest. Seek out a community of faith where a gentle, understanding supportive peer group can be yours. Often a local church can provide you such nurturing people. Maria, there will still be tough times in your life. You're going to need mature Christians to carry you through those rough places. Don't be afraid to ask for help. When crises come, share your burdens; reach out for others' support.

Get some rest at first. There will be plenty of time to labor in your church later on. Don't burn out by accepting too many responsibilities early on. Find a way you can be of service, but avoid taking too much responsibility too soon. Just as the family is the most important group of persons for an infant, your Christian family will be important to you. Christian family members and special Christians in your church will share their experiences in a way that will help you to grow as a new Christian. May your church family indeed be mature.

As you grow in the faith, there are a few exercises that will assist you on your spiritual journey. First, develop a habit of daily prayer. Prayer edifies a Christian. However you begin talking with God, understand that prayer also is listening. As you approach God, express your thanksgiving, your thoughts, your feelings, and then listen. Be still before God, and wait on His word. Maintaining silence before God acknowledges that you know that God is indeed Lord. Listen with your mind, but also listen with your heart.

Maria, a second exercise involves talking about your up's and down's along the pathway to Christian maturity. Right now I imagine that life is joyous, exciting, and filled with a new awareness of peace. But there will still be some dark times when life does not feel so great. Even Christians have bad days! You may be tempted to turn your back on Jesus during those first down times. Don't. Rather, attempt to share your struggles with other Christian pilgrims. Invite someone to walk with you as you search through the darkness. Be assured of God's presence, even in the shadowy experience of life. These up's and down's are a part of spiritual maturity.

Third, share your faith with others. Your witness can be a life-changing power to someone else. You may not know and understand all that the Bible has to say, but your personal story will speak volumes to them. As you grow spiritually, others will want to listen to your story.

Finally, let go of your bad habits. This will not be easy, but you need to get started at the very first. Changing one's negative habits is important to avoid being a negative witness or a stumbling block to others. It is also important that you cast off these bad habits so there will be room in your life for the good. Whenever possible, avoid tempting situations in the first place. And in the second place, replace these old habits with new, more fruitful ones. Don't be afraid to continue to confess your struggle and shortcomings. These bad habits won't disappear all at once.

Maria, this letter may seem so packed with advice that it leaves your head swimming. That won't surprise me. I hope you will keep it and reread it, and that you will begin to keep your own journal as a day-by-day record of how you grow into the Christian young woman God is calling you to be. As you write your story, my prayer is that you will know more fully the story of the Lord Jesus Christ.

Concluding Thought

May the ideas set forth in this book now ferment along with your own collection of adolescents' stories to produce new resources for youth. I challenge you to offer your stories to the teens in your world as a gift from God.

Bibliography

Aleshire, Dan. *Understanding Today's Youth.* Nashville: Broadman Press, 1982.

Berne, Eric. *Games People Play.* New York: Grove Press, 1964.

Burns, David. *Feeling Good: The New Mood Therapy.* New York: Signet Books, 1980.

Clinebell, Howard. *Basic Types of Pastoral Care and Counseling.* rev. ed. Nashville: Abingdon Press, 1984.

Elkind, David. *All Grown Up and No Place to Go: Teenagers in Crisis.* Reading, Mass.: Addison-Wesley Publishing Co., 1964.

_____. *The Hurried Child Growing Up Too Fast Too Soon.* Reading, Mass.: Addison-Wesley Publishing Co., 1981.

Fowler, James. *Stages of Faith.* New York: Harper & Row, 1981.

Group for the Advancement of Psychiatry. *Normal Adolescence.* New York: Charles Scribner's Sons, 1968.

Henderson, Larry. "Determining and Developing a Strategy for Expanding Religious and Moral Awareness with Residents of Arkansas Youth Service Center at Pine Bluff, Arkansas." D.Min. project, The Southern Baptist Theological Seminary, 1977.

Kohlberg, Lawrence. *Moral Development.* Cambridge, Mass.: Harvard Press, 1974.

Kohlberg, Lawrence; Kauffman, Kelsey; Scharf, Peter; and Hickey, Joseph, editors. *The Just Community Approach to Corrections: A Manual, Part 2.* Moral Education for Research Foundation, 1971.

Mother Teresa of Calcutta. *Love for Unborn Children: A Straight Word to Kids and Parents.* Nappanee, Ind.: Evangel Press, 1987.

Nichols, Sue. *Words on Target.* Nashville: Broadman Press, 1978.

Ross, Richard, and Rowatt, G. Wade. *Ministry with Youth and Their Parents.* Nashville: Convention Press, 1986.

Rowatt, G. Wade. *Pastoral Care with Adolescents in Crisis.* Louisville: Westminster/John Knox Press, 1989.

Stinnett, Nicholas. "Strong Families." In *Marriage and Family in a Changing Society.* 2d ed., edited by James N. Henslin. New York: Free Press, 1985.

Strommen, Merton. *Five Cries of Youth.* New York: Harper & Row, 1974.

Wink, Walter. *Transforming Bible Study.* Nashville: Abingdon Press, 1980.

Wynn, J. C. *Family Therapy in Pastoral Ministry.* San Francisco: Harper & Row, 1982.